Grief

Unwrapped

Discovering Joy in a Season of Sorrow

Patricia Cameron

GREEN
LEAF
INK

Green Leaf Ink

ISBN: 979-8-9869673-0-1 (printed softcover)

ISBN: 979-8-9869673-1-8 (printed hardback)

ISBN: 979-8-9869673-2-5 (eBook)

ISBN: 979-8-9869673-3-2 (limited edition printed hardback)

Cover design by Jason Byron Nelson

Editing by Kathie Scriven and Betsy St. Amant

Proofreading by Lauren Cassel Brownell

Typesetting by Patricia Cameron

Find out more at www.patriciacameronwrites.com.

Contents

For His Glory

and

in loving memory of
Matthew Stevens Cameron,
the one who made me laugh

Foreword

I've heard it said that if you want to help someone who is bleeding, you must be willing to hemorrhage a great deal yourself. Patricia Cameron has done just that in Grief Unwrapped.

Following the sudden death of her husband, Patricia faced the biggest trial of her life. And came face to face with whether or not she would trust God.

Patricia's vulnerability has provided us with purposeful truths – in the process of grief. We don't like the process, but the purpose restores us.

When I received Patricia's manuscript, I finished reading it in less than two days! I didn't want to put it down because she grabbed my heart, and she opened her life to deep places of the soul. She understands our bleeding, our hurts and our losses.

Each page hit a nerve within my own losses, hurts and griefs, past and present. This Minister of Encouragement needed Patricia Cameron's encouragement and affirmation. And she delivered it in an Unwrapped fashion indeed.

This book is the one you will want to read often, for life demands it. And you will need more than one copy so you can send it to a friend who is grieving, someone who is bleeding and needs a transfusion of personal, Biblical and practical truth.

Thank you, Patricia, for coming alongside of us — sharing with us and investing in us with your wounds, grief and victories. Thank you for Unwrapping Grief for me.

Dr. Dennis Swanberg
America's Minister of Encouragement
dennisswanberg.com

INTRODUCTION

Dear friends,

Have you ever heard the phrase "suffering tends to make us bitter or better?" Some people leave their faith. Others become complacent. Still others dig in and grow deeper in their relationship with God.

I admit — the sudden loss of my husband did not bring about thoughts of joy. Growing closer to Christ was not even on my radar. Raising three boys alone — boys who needed their daddy — drove me to my knees as my heart ached and loneliness set in.

Through it all, God brought moments of joy to me even in the middle of my hurting. Over time, I learned that God still had more for me to accomplish in my life.

For those on this grief journey, you know that heartache and sadness can overwhelm and stop us in our tracks. Not only do we grieve the death of our spouse, but we grieve the death of our hopes and dreams as well — especially for those who have lost spouses in mid-life or even early senior years.

Through my experiences, as well as those of other widows, I have learned that there is hope when we put our faith and trust in the One who teaches us how to:

- live an abundant life of joy

- find the courage to live beyond the pain

- experience peace by letting go

With God's help, we don't just live to survive. We can learn to thrive and enjoy life again. While loss is not a gift, we can focus on the gift of time we had with our spouse and not on the future we lost.

This book is a collection of thoughts, journal entries and stories not only for the widow but also for her friends and family. After all, it's friends and family who are there to help us on our journey so that we ultimately come out on the other side experiencing the abundant life Jesus promised.

I don't pretend to be an authority on grief, but I lived it. Besides losing my husband when he was 45 (and I was 51), I lost a nephew when he was six, experienced four miscarriages, lost a baby at birth, and lost my best friend to cancer.

I pray God would use whatever pain and whatever lessons I have learned through my own grief to help you as well. My desire is the words on these pages point you to Jesus and give you hope and comfort as you grieve the loss of your spouse.

I pray these words will inspire you to walk through the next days or months or years with a new set of eyes —eyes that see life from God's grand, eternal perspective.

I pray this book will:

- help you move through the grief process,

- point you to God who can heal your broken heart,

- encourage you to strengthen your relationship with God, and

- inspire you to live a life of fullness.

I want to offer to those of you who are still in the stages of intense grief: the pain does ease over time. Today I pray that the words in this book will help you navigate the loneliness, the questions, and a host of seesaw emotions. I pray you will press on to accomplish what God has called you to do — whether it's simply taking care of your children's basic needs, excelling in your job, or taking the time to help others.

Although this may be a difficult season, you can get through it. God has a full life for you. It is my hope that as you turn the pages of this book, you will discover the same joy in your own life. A joy that is grounded in faith in the Lord Jesus Christ.

I hope that a year from now, five years from now, or even 10, you'll look back on this season of suffering and see how God brought joy into your life, and how He enabled you to see beyond the pain to the goodness, peace, and purpose He offers every day.

With love and joy,
Patricia

"These things I have spoken to you, that my joy may remain in you and that your joy may be full." John 15:11

Part 1

---------●---------

Live your Life to the Full

1

"I Love You"

Pour out your hearts to him, for
God is our refuge. Psalm 62:8

I heard the whoosh of the mattress as weight lifted from the other side of the bed.

The bathroom door closed and a few minutes later, my husband walked out ready for a morning run with his buddies from work.

"I love you," he stopped to tell me on his way out of the room.

Those were the last words he ever spoke to me. I will always treasure them and hold them close to my heart. That tragic morning of September 11, 2015, was the trajectory that changed our lives forever.

Matthew rode his bike to the local high school track and told his friends he felt great. At almost one lap, they found him collapsed and unresponsive. In the darkness of that morning, the wait for the ambulance seemed like hours.

Shortly after the ambulance arrived, his boss, Derek, and wife Olga, who were also friends and neighbors, stood outside my front door. He was there to rush me to the hospital. She was there to be with our boys when they woke up.

As Derek and I sped through the city park on the way to the hospital, I thought I wouldn't survive the trip. We must have maxed out the speedometer, arriving several minutes ahead of the ambulance.

We waited outside the emergency room doors. I will never, ever forget the scene as they unloaded my husband while continuing to simultaneously perform procedures. A sense of dread took over, a feeling unlike anything I had ever experienced.

It would be hours before I could even see him again.

While we waited in ICU, he had another episode. From that point on, the goal was to get him stable and see how much damage had been done. The doctors called it an electric event and assured me he never knew what hit him.

Five days

It took five days for the medical staff to perform all the procedures to give Matthew every chance of recovering. But he did not recover. In the end, there was no brain activity. He was gone.

At 51 years old with a 13-, 10- and 8-year-old, I was not equipped for life without my spouse. He had been my partner, my best friend, my top encourager, and the one who challenged me to do my best and to think differently. Each day, I encouraged our boys to pray believing that their dad would get better. They were shocked the day I told them the news.

What had just happened? What was God thinking? I needed my husband. I mean, *really* needed him. And our boys needed their daddy. He was the rock of our family.

Through Matthew's life and death, the Lord taught me that He is the source of true joy. Through the next painful days, He was the rock, the shelter, the provider I needed. He demonstrated His love for me and stood right beside me.

My husband, Matthew Stevens Cameron, lived a life of joy. He kept us laughing and kept us going. He was the life of the party, creative and quick-witted. He loved giving gifts. Even in his death, he gave to others as he donated his organs.

I heard countless stories of how Matthew had influenced and encouraged others, people who had seen something special in him. His cousin, Randall, wrote a social post that I think pretty much covered it.

My cousin, Matthew Cameron, was indeed "one of the crazy ones." Though we will miss him terribly, I feel certain that he died with no regrets. No one in his life had to wonder if he loved them, because it shined through in everything he did. And his memorial service was almost as joyous as his life was. It was a wonderful time with family under tragic circumstances, but there was so much more laughing than crying. Even in death, he set an example of good living. Three things I want to take from Matthew's example:

1. *Love everyone and put your family first.*

2. *Take more photos with the grown-ups in them.*

3. *Do it while you can because tomorrow's not promised.*

2

FIND JOY IN THE JOURNEY

*"I have come that you might have
life and have it to the full." John
10:10*

Widow.

I despise that word because of the irreversible effect it has had on my life.

Years ago, when I went through a divorce, I despised that word too. At the time, it was the worst thing that had ever happened to me. I never wanted it. Fought against it. But it did happen, and I felt the stigma of that word for many years.

I had experienced loss before losing my husband. In addition to the unwanted divorce, my family experienced the brutal murder of my six-year-old nephew. I lost my best friend to cancer and my infant baby to Potter's Syndrome. As painful as these times were, they did not prepare me for the devastation brought on by the loss of my husband. The love of my life and a great father to our three sons, I never could have imagined the rest of my days without him.

Until then, I never knew that a heart could physically ache from grief. I didn't know that I could miss someone with my every breath.

Living Fully Alive

As I have grieved, I've also been reminded of one of my favorite verses. Odd that it's about living a full life. Jesus told us that He came that we might live abundantly. (John 10:10) Not just live, but live life to the full. Not half alive, but fully alive.

For most of my life, that is how I've tried to live. One of my favorite lines from the movie "Ever After," the **Grand Dame said at the end:** "And, while Cinderella and her prince did live happily ever after, the point, gentlemen, is that they *lived*."

I think I got this drive for a full life from my dad. At 89 years old, he decided he would take his three-wheeler for a spin down the street. (Yes, it is a 1980's three-wheeler, not the safer, more stable four-wheeler version. I grew up doing wheelies on that ATV!) His excursion may not sound odd but with two prosthetic legs and at his age, we help him in and out of the car at every outing.

"Dad," I asked, "How did you even manage to get up on the three-wheeler?" He smiled and explained that he had backed up to the seat, pushed himself up, and swung one leg over. I think his drive to prove he could do it, along with sheer determination, got him on and off it! My heart races just thinking about it.

Nothing like living life to the fullest, right? He says that when he turns 90, he'll probably stop doing stuff like that. (He hit the milestone shortly before this book was published.) We still have to reign him in from time to time.

That's the way I want to live the rest of my days. Maybe not breaking the law, but really living. I think Jesus would have us do the same thing and live a life overflowing with joy. After all, the Bible teaches He is the source of all joy.

Living in Survival Mode

However, being honest with myself, I have lived mostly in survival mode since my husband passed away at 45, after almost 20 years of marriage. Years before, I remember thinking that if something ever happened to me, he would be fine without me. But if the situation were reversed, I wouldn't be able to handle it. I would be lost without him.

Maybe continuing in survival mode is just part of going through the grieving process. Because our children were younger when he passed away, all my energy became focused on them. At their young ages and with their many activities, I never took the time to participate in any type of grief therapy or counseling. I certainly encourage attending grief therapy classes; I know of many who have benefited greatly from them. But in that season, I didn't think I could spare the time.

Every journey is unique. No two experiences will be the same, but we can all learn from each other. People often told me they didn't know how I did it—managing the loss of my husband on top of the responsibility of taking care of our three sons.

But what other choice do we have when people depend on us? We survive to make sure they have as normal a childhood as possible.

I do know that there came a point when I didn't want to be in that place anymore. I wanted to live fully aware of God's presence, His power and the work He was — and is continuing to do — in my life.

The Dilemma?

Here's the dilemma. How do we live with joy when our hearts are broken? When we're buried beneath a mountain of shock and grief? When there's a knot in the pit of our stomach that won't go away? When we can't catch our breath and our bodies are numb, our energy diminished? When our hearts are heavy and we're bone-tired and weary?

How do we live with joy when running across an old email from our late spouse makes us miss them even more? Where is joy when we don't know what we're doing and feel like a failure with our kids? Or when the doctor's office calls to confirm our spouse's next appointment and we have to tell them the news?

Two days before my husband's memorial service, our house turned into a flurry of activity with friends and family. Caught up in the task of getting photos selected for the service, I automatically asked one of the boys to "run upstairs to tell daddy" something. As my child looked at me absently, I realized my mistake — he was gone.

We mourn for our children's absence of an earthy father, the absence of his influence. How do we recognize their pain when we don't even know how to deal with our own?

Returning home after a short trip a few months later, I walked into the bedroom and smelled my husband's cologne. And long after he was gone, I discovered my boys had been secretly calling his phone number just to hear his voice.

Where is joy when you come up empty after searching for passwords to online accounts? Or when your wedding anniversary draws near and you want to dig a hole and hide? When your child tells you his new year's wish because he knows it won't come true-his daddy's not coming back.

What do you do when joy and laughter have been absent from your home for a really long time?

And then when we do have happy moments and good days, we tend to feel shame as if we're not allowed to enjoy anything after what happened to our spouse. We desperately want normal, but normal escapes us.

How do we learn to dig our way out and thrive, not just survive?

Living to Thrive

The only way I know how to answer this question is through the love of God, the grace of God, and the Word of God.

THE LOVE OF GOD

I once knew someone whose husband had been gone for a very long time. She never remarried. Instead, she always said that God was her husband. I'll admit, I never related to her comment. Prone to become dependent on the other person in my relationship, I couldn't imagine feeling that way about the Lord. I get what she was saying — I believe she meant God taking care of her, filling in the void in her life. However, I consider God's love more like a father than a husband.

God is God and He loves us, and I receive great satisfaction and fulfillment from my relationship with Him. But that is not the same thing as having another human being as a partner in life, someone to hold and talk to.

Jeremiah says that God's love is everlasting.

I have loved you with an everlasting love. Jeremiah 31:3

God is so much more than a husband. We cannot even fathom the heart of God. The only comparison that even comes close is a parent's love for a child.

I absolutely love, love, love watching my boys have a good time. Pulling my son and his friend on a tube around the lake one holiday weekend, the joy on their faces put joy in my heart. I love doing things for them and love it when they are happy. Don't you think God feels that way when we're having pure, clean fun? I left that day with windblown hair and the lingering effects of the sun on my face, thanking God for those moments.

His love is incomprehensible, boundless. His faithfulness is indescribable, never-ending.

The love of Jesus carries me through everything in every circumstance. According to the Apostle Paul, nothing can separate us from the love of God.

For I am convinced that neither death nor life, neither angels nor demons, neither the present nor the future, nor any powers, neither height nor depth, nor anything else in all creation will be able to separate us from the love of God that is in Christ Jesus our Lord. Romans 8:38-39

THE GRACE OF GOD

The love of God and the grace of God go hand-in-hand. You cannot experience the grace of God without also experiencing the love of God. You cannot truly love someone without showing them grace. I'm sure I said a few unkind words to people who loved me and tried to help me through my grief. But simple understanding and grace was extended to me.

Grace is undeserved favor.

God not only provided people to extend grace to me, but He also provided the strength to take one step at a time. He supplies exactly the amount of strength we need to make it through the next day. As God's children, we can approach Him and find grace to help us in our time of need. We can come boldly before God's throne because of the name of Jesus.

Let us then approach God's throne of grace with confidence, so that we may receive mercy and find grace to help us in our time of need. Hebrews 4:16

Let us also extend grace and pray for others too. Consider Job's story. After he prayed for his friends, the Lord restored Job's prosperity.

After Job had prayed for his friends, the LORD restored his fortunes and gave him twice as much as he had before. Job 42:10

THE WORD OF GOD

Sometimes feeling God's love during different seasons in our lives is difficult at best. We must lean into the Word of God, believing what it says. The Bible teaches that the source of all joy is Jesus.

So while we may not always *feel* joy, we can have inner joy through faith in Jesus Christ.

When Jesus spoke again to the people, he said, "I am the light of the world. Whoever follows me will never walk in darkness, but will have the light of life." John 8:12

David also expressed his source of joy. He wrote "You make known to me the path of life; in your presence there is fullness of joy; at your right hand are pleasures forevermore." (Psalm 16:11)

Jesus tells us "I have come that they might have life, and have it to the full." John 10:10

That scripture tells us that Jesus doesn't just want us to get through this life . . but to enjoy it and live a fulfilling and gratifying life. While there will be sad moments, those should not characterize our lives. Our lives should have many moments full of love and laughter that we will treasure for years to come.

Jesus Himself showed us how to live a full life. He attended weddings, He cared for people, He loved on children, He went away to rest and refresh Himself, He prayed, He told stories, He wept and suffered. He did what was right no matter what people thought of Him. He loved us to the point of dying for us.

Also in John 10:10, Jesus reminds us that the thief comes to steal and kill and destroy. That same enemy, Satan, wants to steal our joy and to rob us of the gift of knowing Christ. He wants to destroy our faith and have us feel hopeless and bound. He wants us to experience feelings of negativity, including doubt that God really loves us.

The first lying spirit — the serpent in the Garden of Eden — caused Adam and Eve to doubt God's Word. He lied about the goodness of God when he suggested that God was holding out on them. For every 500 lying voices out there, there's one telling you the truth.

That one is found through the Word of God.

REMEMBER HIS PROMISES

How do we know which voice is speaking the truth? Do we tend to hear only what we want to hear? We can recognize truth when it is consistent with the Word of God.

Get to know God by spending time with Him. His Word is filled with words of encouragement, hope and promise. It tells us that Jesus sets us free and gives us hope for a full life.

Even in our grief, we can start by remembering His promises and cherishing the years we had with our spouse. Moments of celebration and laughter. Moments of awe and wonder. Moments of an incredible God expressing his love and beauty.

Let's put our hope in God alone. Listen to His voice. Trusting Him, we will not be shaken.

I keep my eyes always on the LORD. With him at my right hand, I will not be shaken. Psalm 16:8

Living in God's Nearness

Over the years, I have penned experiences that have reminded me that God was near. I know I have missed capturing them many times, but I am thankful for the times I did write them down. These moments remind me that God is with me, even when I don't always "feel" His presence. Remembering these have helped me with the healing process.

Sweet memories are like treasured heirlooms. In those sweet, small moments, we can feel that God is near. It may be that we need to take a moment to breathe, to be still so that we can capture those moments and be reminded that God loves us and expresses His love in all kinds of ways, both big and small.

I once took a mental picture as I watched my husband reading a book to our three boys at bedtime. They were gathered around him looking and listening intently, so sweet and innocent. I wanted to capture that moment. God blessed me that evening, reminding me how sweet life can be and to treasure the everyday and simple snapshots of time in our lives.

Remembering it gives me joy.

What does joy look like to you? Is it happiness or fulfillment? Is it a sense of purpose or an achievement?

Every widow's journey is unique. Our experiences and our reactions may be different, but when it comes to joy, all believers who have lost spouses have one thing in common and that is Jesus. The source of all joy, peace and contentment is found in Jesus. Being in God's will or living in His purpose for our lives brings joy.

I've always loved the quote by Maya Angelou – "Life is not measured by the number of breaths we take, but by the moments that take our breath away." Life is measured in moments, not time.

I'm not downplaying the heart-wrenching moments when we see a loved one slowly deteriorate from cancer or experience a sudden death or the illness or circumstance that took them from this world. I experienced plenty of those while sitting beside my husband for five days in the hospital. But as God brings good memories to mind, take the time not only to remember but to cherish them as gifts from God.

Allow yourself to remember. It may just help you experience God's nearness and find joy in the journey.

BEING HELD

About a year and a half after Matthew's death, God showed me what it was like to be held by Him. That night had been a particularly rough one for me. Missing my husband, I cried out to God that I wished I could be held by my husband again. For 19 years, I had had someone to talk to about my day, the boys' activities, family, and work-related topics. I missed him.

God has His way of meeting our needs. I couldn't sleep. As I lay there, I became very still. So still that my right hand felt swollen from lying in the same position for a while. It felt as if someone was holding my hand. I lay there completely still because I didn't want to lose that moment.

The next night my youngest son ended up in my bed and as he got settled, he asked "Mommy, can I hold your hand?" So, we held hands.

Another sleepless night followed. I opened my Bible app and started reading the next devotional verse - Psalm 135:14.

Keep trusting in God, For the Lord will vindicate his people, and have compassion on his servants. 'God stands up for his people, God holds the hands of his people.' (Psalm 135:14, MSG Bible)

Wow. Talk about getting my attention. God reminded me, again, that He is real. That He is always near. And that He cares about the small things that speak to us and help us heal.

I am convinced we miss out on many "God moments" that could give us additional strength because we don't recognize them. In Daniel 10:18, Daniel says that when the Lord spoke to him, he was strengthened.

These moments happen around us all the time, whether we experience them or not. Paying attention to them could change the direction of your day. I encourage you to take some time this week to slow down and ask God to show you those moments, ask Him to strengthen you. He's only a whisper away.

So do not fear, for I am with you; do not be dismayed, for I am your God. I will strengthen you and help you; I will uphold you with my righteous hand. Isaiah 41:10

Pray With Me

Lord, your love is boundless, and I know You desire to bring good things to our lives and have us live life to the full even as we grieve. I am thankful for Your love, Your grace and Your word. Thank You for meeting me in my need. You are enough, Lord. Help me to believe this and not go overboard seeking other things or other people to fill the void in my life. Be my all in all, my sustainer. Help me to trust You to meet all my needs in time. In Jesus' name, amen.

———————————— 🎩 ————————————

Questions for Reflection / Thoughts to Ponder

1. What is your survival mode? What is your biggest hindrance to experiencing joy?

2. How have you experienced God's nearness? How has God's love ministered to you? List specific verses that have provided comfort to you in your moments of greatest sadness or emotional pain.

3. Take some time to think about special memories of your loved one that bring you joy.

3

FEEL GOD'S PRESENCE

*You make known to me the path
of life; you will fill me with joy in
your presence, with eternal pleasures at your right hand. Psalm
16:11*

What a day that will be, when my Jesus I shall see.

When I look upon His face, the one who saved me by His grace.

Then He'll take me by the hand, and lead me through the promised land.

What a day, glorious day that will be.

The verses from this old hymn popped into my head as I drove home from a basketball game late one night. This seems to be much of my life with three boys — ballgames and long drives. The moon was out, striking and bright. And there was a multitude of tiny feathery clouds floating over and around it. It made me think of an army of angels gathered around the Father. I attempted to take a picture while driving, but that became almost disastrous, so I pulled over to capture the view.

Moments. I am learning to enjoy moments like these again. Seems I'd lost my way over time, forgetting to enjoy the little things life has to offer. Instead, I allowed the stress of situations around me to consume my mind and thoughts. Although many times I'd asked Jesus to speak to me and show me His presence, I would often miss it. That night, God showed up and I worshipped him in song and enjoyed the brilliance of the moonlit sky above me.

Being in the presence of Jesus encourages us, moves us, changes us, strengthens us, and delivers us.

The Presence of Jesus Encourages You

I was blessed again with another "God moment" the next afternoon. Leaving my home to watch another ballgame — soccer this time — I noticed the sunset was beginning to show its colors. So I took a minute to drive to where I could see it best. The view almost took my breath away. I was caught up in His presence as God painted that sky with breathtaking reds and oranges. The houseboat in the foreground is an added plus!

Something incredible happened as I was editing this section of this chapter. I literally had just read about that fiery sunset when a memory popped up in my photos of that picture — taken exactly one year ago that very day. I have learned to not make assumptions about those moments. What an awesome and loving God we have.

While those moments were bold and beautiful, God also reminded me of His presence with a tiny, but amazing creature. I was surprised and awe-struck by a long-forgotten sight — fireflies at dusk. I wonder what God was thinking when He created their bodies to light up like that. I couldn't get enough, watching outside until the last one lit up. While they weren't colorful, big, or bright and brilliant, these tiny lit creatures reminded me of a simpler time in my life, and again, to stop and enjoy the moment.

I believe God gives us these holy moments to encourage us, to remind us that He will show us His presence, His brilliance, and His peace.

When I look at your heavens, the work of your fingers, the moon and the stars, which you have set in place, what is mankind that

you are mindful of them, human beings that you care for them?
Psalm 8:3-4

Many times, we wander in a sea of restlessness and busyness, allowing it to be a distraction from the pain. Take time to look for those God-given moments. It may be a small moment that could easily be missed. But it is there if we will just slow down long enough to look — or listen.

The Presence of Jesus Moves You

I pray that you, too, will be caught up in His presence in some way. I remember the day I first heard Cody Carnes' song *Nothing Else.* I was moved. It so summed up my thoughts and where I want to be — sitting at the feet of Jesus, caught up in holy moments. The first time I heard it was at a women's day conference at my church.

After that, I couldn't get enough. I would sit and listen as he sang about how he longed to sit with Jesus, not for the blessing of anything except His presence. It captures the struggle we have with going through the motions many times at church and how important it is to go back to where we first started when our hearts were newly opened to Him.

Seek God's presence in good times and in bad. Always.

"Always be on the lookout for the presence of wonder."
E. B. White, American essayist, author and literary stylist, who authored *Charlotte's Web.*

MercyMe's song *Here With Me* paints a beautiful picture of experiencing the presence of the Lord. It describes our longing for God's presence, then being lost in the beauty of His presence. I can picture many times when I have asked God to reveal Himself to me and suddenly I am lost in the beauty of the moment or caught up in the wonder of my surroundings. The song mentions falling down on our knees and feeling the presence of God.

THE HAND OF GOD

Driving home from, yes, yet another soccer tournament, one of my favorite songs was playing on the radio – *In the Waiting* by Greg Long. The lyrics cover wanting to see God's hand move. This song sustained me during the time we waited on our baby girl to be born, knowing she didn't have the organs to live once she was delivered. (During a routine ultrasound at 20 weeks, we learned she would not live once she was born.) Greg Long describes pain as the gift nobody longs for but that leaves us stronger when it's gone.

The song struck me in a different way this time. It goes on to say the hardest part is waiting on God when what I really want is to see His hand move. The lyrics highlight that God's silence doesn't mean that we're alone. As I listened and sang along, I asked God to let me see His hand move.

Call me crazy, but I searched and searched the clouds, trying to see them shaped like God's hand. I saw nothing. I criticized myself for wanting a sign so badly.

God answered that request the next day as I read this verse from Isaiah and sat in awe.

I will not forget you! See, I have engraved you on the palm of my hands. Isaiah 49:15-16.

Not only did God show me that verse, but I read three random verses that day that talked about God's hand at different times. Surely God delights in surprising us through His word. It never disappoints.

The Presence of Jesus Changes You

Just being in the presence of Jesus changes you. It did for Zacchaeus. Before Jesus, Zacchaeus was dishonest and despised by many, cheating his own countrymen by overcharging their tax assessments. When he heard Jesus was passing through Jericho, his curiosity compelled him to see for himself. Maybe it was more than curiosity. Maybe his material wealth failed to satisfy the longing of his soul.

Jesus was looking for Zacchaeus, too, and that one encounter changed his life. When Jesus said he was coming over, Zacchaeus came down at once and welcomed Jesus gladly. He gave half of his possessions to the poor, also giving back over and above what he cheated people.

UNVEILED

Moses was changed after being in the presence of God. After he came from Mount Sinai, he would never be the same. He didn't know that his face was radiant at first. Later, he placed a veil over it because he did not want the Israelites to see that the light that shone on his face was fading away. (Exodus 34.29-30)

Like Moses, we are also changed when we are in the presence of Jesus. We are being transformed into his image.

In the movie *Return to Me,* the main character, Grace, is transformed when her new heart starts beating. It is an incredible thought. I want a heart transplant — not literally, but I want to be transformed spiritually. I want to be so like Jesus that I look, act, and feel different.

In his letter to the Romans, Paul reminds us to be transformed by the renewing of our minds. (Romans 12:2)

Paul also wrote to the Corinthians, reminding them they were being transformed into the Lord's likeness.

But whenever anyone turns to the Lord, the veil is taken away.
Now the Lord is the Spirit, and where the Spirit of the Lord
is, there is freedom. And we all, who with unveiled faces con-
template the Lord's glory, are being transformed into his image
with ever-increasing glory, which comes from the Lord, who is the
Spirit. 2 Corinthians 3:16-18

A man full of faith and of the Holy Spirit, Stephen — a martyr of the church — spoke out against the corruption of temple worship. This provoked the anger of the officials who were profiting from their practices. These men accused Stephen of blasphemy against God and Moses and incited a mob who took him to court. While they observed Stephen in court, his face was described as looking like the face of an angel. Because of this they dragged him out of the city and flung rocks at him. Moments before his death, he described seeing heaven open and the Son of Man standing at the right hand of God. Can you just imagine his face becoming more and more radiant as the pain from the final blow sealed his fate?

When we have been with God, our countenance should look different than those who don't know God.

I want people to see Jesus in me.

As I read about Stephen one morning, I prayed that my countenance would be like Stephen's or Moses' when they had been in the presence of the Lord. Later, as I read a devotion, I wrote down words that stood out to me. Then as I read that morning's note and the afternoon's note together, I recognized that one was an answer to the other! If we want our countenance to reflect Christ, we need to let go of self and let Christ's divine power work through us. As John 3:30 says, He must become greater; I must become less.

The Presence of Jesus Strengthens You

What a tragedy it would be to fall so far away in our relationship with God that we don't realize that the Lord's presence has left us.

Let's take a look at one man's experience from the book of Judges in the Bible. Samson was one of the last judges of Israel. Hebrews lists Samson as one of the heroes of the faith. In a day where evil prevailed, God allowed Samson to lead the Israelites for 20 years, using his God-given physical strength.

Samson knew that his power came from God. His downfall wasn't a lack of faith, but rather, it was in thinking God's power would never leave him, no matter his conduct. He fell in love with a godless woman and abandoned his God-given purpose in life.

Scripture tells us that while Samson was sleeping, his strength left him. When he awoke, he did not know the Lord had left. (Judges 16:20b)

How could that be? When I read the story about Samson and Delilah, her actions practically shouted to Samson that she was selling him out. She asked for the key to Samson's strength. Three times he lied to her. Three times she had the Philistines in her home waiting for him to wake up.

He finally gave in and told her the real reason for his supernatural strength — that if his head were shaved, he'd lose his strength and become as weak as any other man. What did she do? The very same thing as before. Except this time she had his head shaved, then called the Philistines. Samson was powerless. His strength was gone.

To me, the saddest part of this story is that he got up thinking he was strong but didn't realize the Lord had left him.

I pray that that will never be our story. The Bible teaches us that God will never leave us or forsake us. But there are times when we completely miss Him. When we get distracted or busy planning, scheduling, and doing — without the Holy Spirit — we're working in our own strength.

Like Samson, without God's strength, we are weak and powerless to do his will. With His strength, we can stand strong in the midst of everyday trials, pain, and circumstances of life.

The Holy Spirit Comes to Help, Comfort and Defend

In light of Samson's story and the day he lived in, I'm reminded of the fallen world we live in and how desperately we need the presence of the Holy Spirit. After His resurrection but before Jesus ascended to the Father, He promised the disciples that the Holy Spirit would come to help, comfort, and defend them, teaching them what they would need to know.

We need to make a conscious effort to seek His guidance in every area of our lives. Christ will not force His way into our lives. We have to daily, or sometimes hourly, invite Him in.

Growing up, I remember a song we sang about the Holy Spirit, *Come Holy Spirit*. I believe the words speak the truth to us today. The lyrics talk about the darkness around us and how we need God's presence, His love and His power. The song calls to God, asking Him to move and stir the church to experience revival.

Jesus told his disciples it was better that He go away so that the Holy Spirit could come. Get to know this part of the godhead that Jesus referred to as The Comforter. If you let him, He will lead you, guide you, help you, comfort you, and give you strength in the days ahead.

"But the Advocate, the Holy Spirit, whom the Father will send in my name, will teach you all things and will remind you of everything I have said to you. John 14:25-26

The Presence of Jesus Delivers You

God is in both big things and small things.

While sitting on my porch one night, I watched a hummingbird fly up to a plant next to me. He visited every flower on that plant. I marveled that he was so close to me. And then he did the strangest thing. He flew in front of me and hovered for a few heartbeats. It was as if he was looking straight at me.

I got goosebumps all over my body. It certainly got my attention, and I felt God reminding me He reveals His presence in big ways and small ways. But He's always there. Always near.

The point is that we can look for, pray for, and hold onto His presence when it manifests in our lives.

When all is well, our needs tend to be different. We have much to fulfill us and our mind is focused on that next event, the next holiday, the next assignment at work, or the next vacation with our family.

However, in our season of grief, we usually want and need the assurance that God is there. We long to be reminded that He has not forsaken us or left us. Although it may seem that way for a time, He will ultimately deliver us.

THE HOLY SPIRIT MEETS US IN THE ROUTINE

As part of her routine walk to the town well, a Samaritan woman experienced being in the actual presence of Jesus.

When Jesus stopped at a well in Samaria on His way to Galilee, He met her there. Sometimes, Jesus has to get right in our faces for us to get it. John 4:25 says that the woman knew that the Messiah (called Christ) was coming and that He would explain everything when He came.

Then Jesus declared, "I the one speaking to you — I am he." John 4:26

It took her a minute, but when she got it — when the lightbulb came on — she got it. She left for town and told the people who she had seen. Many believed because of her testimony.

The Lord blessed her that day with His presence. When He did, she went out and blessed others. So I encourage you to look for the moments, celebrate them, and share them with others so they can be encouraged as well.

Our God of the universe is also God of the details. Don't miss the beauty of flowers or nature around you. His hand paints brilliant sunsets, yet He's also in our quiet moments. He is our deliverer, our healer. He can deliver us from this season of pain.

He uses little things to accomplish the big. He is at work in all things — in a routine task, and even in a tiny bird's visit.

We can have confidence in His presence, even when we hear no voice. There is no greater joy than being in the presence of the Lord. Rest in that presence.

———————————— 🎩 ————————————

Pray With Me

Lord Jesus, help me to slow down so I don't miss the beauty of this life and You in it, and even of this season. Remove any barriers and usher me into Your presence. Order my steps so I am right where You want me to be. Walking in Your presence is better than anything I could gain or do during my day. Help me to live today as a testimony of Your presence in my life. I want to always be on the lookout for the presence of wonder. In Jesus' name, amen.

In your presence there is fullness of joy Psalm 16:11 (ESV)

Be still in the presence of the Lord, and wait patiently for Him to act. Psalm 37:7 (NLT)

Lift up your eyes and look to the heavens: Who created all these? He who brings out the starry host one by one and calls forth each of them by name. Because of his great power and mighty strength, not one of them is missing. Isaiah 40:26

I can never escape from your Spirit! I can never get away from your presence! If I go up to heaven, you are there; If I go down to the grave, you are there. Psalm 139:7-8 (NLT)

God has said, "Never will I leave you; never will I forsake you." Hebrews 13:5

Questions for Reflection / Thoughts to Ponder

1. Think about the times when you felt God's presence the strongest. Think about what you were doing, and how it made you feel. Write them down.

2. How do you think we miss out on God moments? What can you do to savor and remember them?

3. Think about a time when you saw God use small things in your life to accomplish something bigger.

4

FUELED BY THE POWER OF THE HOLY SPIRIT

*I am going to send you what my
Father has promised; but stay in
the city until you have been clothed
with power from on high. Luke
24:49*

T here is pow'r, pow'r, wonder-working pow'r.

In the blood of the Lamb.
There is pow'r, pow'r, wonder-working pow'r
In the precious blood of the lamb.

These few lines from a well-known gospel hymn, *There's Power in the
Blood,* speak to God's wonder-working power. The power of the Lord
knows no limit. We should never attempt to limit it.

Even when we're out of strength, not sure how we'll manage the next hour, let alone the next day, God's power is sufficient.

Have you ever pushed through something, letting nothing stand in your way?

RUN THE RACE

At my husband's encouragement Thanksgiving Day in 2014, I ran a local Turkey Trot, a 2-mile race, with my middle son, Garrett. My husband suggested it was something the two of us could do together. He, conveniently, stayed home in the warm house with the other two boys.

Garrett was nine at the time and it was his first race. He didn't want to run the whole course by himself and asked me to keep up with him. I knew he could run faster than me, but I gave it my best shot.

With my eyes on my son, nothing could stand in my way . . . except the second mile. I ran as fast as I'd ever run (well, at least since college), but finally lost sight of him. I'm glad he felt confident to keep running without me.

My reward, other than seeing his accomplishment? I won the Female Grand Masters category, which I never would have done if I hadn't been trying to keep up! At least they didn't include my age on the award. Being in the Grand Masters category was embarrassing enough!

Elijah, a prophet in Israel, presented a challenge to King Ahab, an evil king who did more to provoke the Lord to anger than all the kings of Israel who were before him. (1 Kings 16:30, 33)

Ahab called Elijah the troubler of Israel. There was no love lost between the two. Elijah challenged Ahab to bring all the Israelites and all the prophets of Baal and Ashera to Mt. Carmel. Two altars were built. Ahab's prophets were to call on the name of their god, and Elijah would call on the name of the Lord. Elijah said the god who answered by fire was God.

In the end, Elijah's God sent fire from heaven that lapped up everything — the sacrifice, the wood, the stones and soil, and even the water in the trench.

There was no question about who God was.

After the Lord defeated the prophets of Baal, Elijah suggested Ahab head back to the city before the rain could stop him. Here's the interesting part.

The power of the Lord came upon Elijah and he ran ahead of Ahab. Ahab was in a chariot. With God's power as his fuel, nothing could stop or stand in Elijah's way.

Meanwhile, the sky grew black with clouds, the wind rose, a heavy rain started falling and Ahab rode off to Jezreel. The power of the Lord came on Elijah and, tucking his cloak into his belt, he ran ahead of Ahab all the way to Jezreel. 1Kings 18:45-46

Since I lost my husband, there have been countless times that I have cried out to God "I can't do this!" yet with the power of the Holy Spirit, I would pick myself back up and take the next step, and then the next and next.

There was a point in time when I thought I simply couldn't go on. We were approaching the one-year anniversary of Matthew's death. A few days before the anniversary, I was invited to attend a women's retreat. That weekend was the most spiritually moving experience of my life. God provided healing and comfort through a group of ladies who allowed themselves to be used by Him, who allowed the power of the Holy Spirit to work in them, and I began to hope again.

As Christians, *we would do well to remember that the same Spirit that raised Christ from the dead lives in us*. The Holy Spirit is a vital and equal part of the Trinity, promised to believers. Intellectually, we know that the Holy Spirit equips us with strength and the power to do the things we have been called to do. But do we really believe it?

Two things are essential to living out our calling or our purpose. Our faith and God's power. I want my faith to be fueled by the power of the Holy Spirit.

I believe that living in the power of the Holy Spirit requires obedience, a daily walk with God, and total dependence on Him.

Obedience

We can't expect to live in the power of the Holy Spirit if we're not being obedient.

And receive from him anything we ask, because we obey his commands and do what pleases him. 1 John 3:22

God clearly spoke to me about my need to respond to a situation that was heavy on my mind. It wasn't the response I wanted to make or had planned to make at the time, but I knew in my heart that it would be clear disobedience if I did it my way. At that moment, God impressed upon me that if I wanted to walk in the power of the Holy Spirit, I needed to respond His way.

> Author A. W. Tozer said "A Christian cannot hope for the true manifestation of God while he lives in a state of disobedience. Let a man refuse to obey God on some point, and the rest of his religious activity will be wasted."
> ([1])

Jesus gave us a perfect example of being submissive to God's will. In His prayer in the Garden of Gethsemane, Jesus asked the Father if He could skip going through the agonizing and painful trial of dying on a cross. However, He concluded He would trust His Heavenly Father and do His Father's will, not His own.

Even godly men in the Bible disobeyed. Take King David for example. The Bible describes David as a man after God's own heart. Let's take a look at how his disobedience negatively affected many.

THE GREAT COVER-UP

But David remained in Jerusalem. 2 Samuel 11:1

David wasn't where he was supposed to be on a particular night. Because of that, he saw something he wasn't supposed to see - Bathsheba bathing. Because of that, he acted on a sinful desire and had sexual relations with her.

Because David remained in Jerusalem:

- A husband and soldier lost his life in battle;

- A woman became a widow; and

- A baby died.

But God still used David and even called him a man after His own heart.

Even when we sin, and we and others suffer as a result of that sin, God can still use us.

A MATTER OF THE HEART

It's a matter of the heart.

When my oldest son, Connor, was four, he told me his heart was broken and he needed a new one. Curious, I asked him who could give him a new heart and he replied, "Jesus."

We all could learn from that. When we sin, we need to ask for forgiveness and believe God will cleanse us and purify our hearts.

David was a great example of this. Over and over, we see him walking in obedience, and in the power of His God. Scripture often speaks of David's faithfulness. We are told that David did what was right in the eyes of the Lord and had not failed to keep any of the Lord's commandments, except in the area of Uriah the Hittite. (1 Kings 15:5)

God used David in many ways, particularly through his writings in Psalms. His son, Solomon, was also a great king and honored the Lord in many significant ways.

May we learn and accept that kind of faith. Obey God and when we fail, which we all will do from time to time, seek forgiveness and strive to obey going forward.

A Daily Walk With God

Walking daily with God, studying scripture, praying, and meditating are key to living in the power of the Holy Spirit. One of my favorite stories in the Bible is about Enoch.

As the story in Genesis goes, Enoch walked with God. One day, God decided He wanted Enoch to be with Him so he took him from this life. (Genesis 5:24) No death. No burial. God just took him. I wonder what that must have felt like. God was so pleased with Enoch that He spared him from death and immediately took him away.

The book of Hebrews confirms Enoch's story.

By faith Enoch was taken from this life, so that he did not experience death: "He could not be found, because God had taken him away." For before he was taken, he was commended as one who pleased God. Hebrews 11:5

We can also learn from Abraham, who also walked daily with God. He considered God to be faithful who had made him the promise that he would become a father, even in his old age.

According to the book of Romans, Abraham never wavered in believing God's promise. In fact, his faith grew stronger, and he gave glory to God.

Don't miss this. As his faith grew stronger, Abraham brought glory to God. The reverse is also true. As we praise God, our faith will increase. (Romans 4:20)

As I have cried out to God for strength, I have grown closer to Him.

The path of a widow is not easy. Some days, it's quite an effort just to get out of bed. For most of us, our lives have suddenly changed from discussing and making decisions together to bearing full responsibility for our family and our finances.

Our daily walk with God strengthens our faith and empowers us to walk in the power of the Holy Spirit.

KEEPING OUR BALANCE

On Christ the solid rock I stand,
  all other ground is sinking sand.
  All other ground is sinking sand.

The words of this well-known hymn, *The Solid Rock,* tell us of the importance of keeping our focus on Christ.

Our daily walk needs focus. It needs balance.

If you're familiar with riding a stand-up paddle board, you know the importance of balance. Appearing much like a surfboard, a paddleboard involves standing up on a board and using a paddle to make your way through the water.

We need our feet firmly planted to achieve balance on a paddle board as well as in life. I learned that lesson the hard way on both counts. Not quite steady on my new board, I put it in the lake early enough to beat the boaters. Boats with motors create waves and waves make keeping your balance tough. Boaters aren't worried about your balance. They're just out there to have fun, too.

But the boaters showed up early as I did. That day, I learned that by keeping your body flexible while your feet are planted, you can weather the waves.

You may be going through your day feeling confident on your feet, only to have one word trigger waves of grief. Sometimes, just seeing a post of other couples enjoying a vacation together stings your heart.

With a solid foundation through our faith and trust in Jesus, we can withstand whatever the day brings. Not that it will be easy, and we might lose our balance for a time. But we've got to get back up on that board, enjoy the sun and breeze on our faces . . . and ride.

The Power that Sustains Us

Christ, our solid rock, is the power that we need to keep our balance and make it through our storm.

Peter learned that firsthand. On a boat with other disciples, he saw Jesus walking on the water. In his enthusiasm, he stepped out of the boat and walked toward Jesus. Losing his focus for a moment, he started sinking and reached out to grab Jesus' hand.

Just like Peter stretching out his hand for Jesus, we can be sure Jesus is there and His power will sustain us, despite any turbulence we may encounter. He also wants to strengthen our faith. He wants us to depend on Him and His strength in our times of weakness.

Many times we think about Peter's lack of faith when we think about his walk on water. However, he did show faith the moment he stepped out. It was when he began to focus on the distractions, rather than on Jesus, that he began to sink. But you have to give him credit. He at least got out of the boat! If we don't get out of the boat, we'll never walk on water.

Matthew 14 gives us the full account.

"Lord, if it's you," Peter replied, "tell me to come to you on the water." "Come," he said. Then Peter got down out of the boat, walked on the water and came toward Jesus. But when he saw the wind, he was afraid and, beginning to sink, cried out, "Lord, save me!" Immediately Jesus reached out his hand and caught him. "You of little faith," he said, "why did you doubt?" And when they climbed into the boat, the wind died down. Then those who were in the boat worshiped him, saying, "Truly you are the Son of God." Matthew 14:28-33

MANAGING OUR EXPECTATIONS

For Spring Break with my boys one year, I booked a condo with a "gulf view" room. In case you haven't figured it out yet, marketing can be deceptive. While sitting on the living room couch in the condo, I could actually see the Gulf of Mexico. But that required looking in between another 16-floor condo, through some power lines, and across the street! Not really close enough to feel the sweet salty air on my face. Not close enough to hear the roar of the waves crashing inland. Not exactly what I had in mind.

Our view of God can be distorted sometimes, too. We know He's out there. I mean, He's almighty God. He's all-powerful and ever-present. He is the Creator and sustainer of the universe, the Great I am, our King of Kings. But are we close enough to feel his presence? Are we close enough to hear His voice?

Do we spend enough time with Him to learn what His voice sounds like? What do the Holy Spirit's leading and impressions feel like?

Let's take a look at what the prophet Elijah's expectations were regarding hearing from God. He had fled from the evil Queen Jezebel, arriving at Horeb. There the Lord asked what he was doing there, then told him to stand on the mountain and wait for Him to pass by. Elijah expected to hear from God in the mighty wind that tore the mountains apart, or in the earthquake or fire that came next, but he didn't. It was in stillness, with a gentle whisper, that he heard from God.

The Lord said, "Go out and stand on the mountain in the presence of the Lord, for the Lord is about to pass by."

Then a great and powerful wind tore the mountains apart and shattered the rocks before the Lord, but the Lord was not in the wind. After the wind there was an earthquake, but the Lord was not in the earthquake. After the earthquake came a fire, but the Lord was not in the fire. And after the fire came a gentle whisper. When Elijah heard it, he pulled his cloak over his face and went out and stood at the mouth of the cave. 1 Kings 19:11-13

And my friend, that's the way it is for us. If we want to hear from God, we need to be close enough, be still enough, and with a great enough desire to hear and listen. Then we will experience that closeness we long to have. When we draw closer to God, seeking Him with all our hearts, we will feel His presence once again.

Come near to God and he will come near to you. James 8:10

Listen to my instruction and be wise; do not disregard it. Blessed are those who listen to me, watching daily at my doors, waiting at my doorway. For those who find me find life and receive favor from the Lord. Proverbs 8:33-35

We are blessed when we maintain a daily walk and listen to God.

Total Dependence on God

It is in our dependence on God that we see Him.

To depend on God means fully trusting in Him to supply all our needs. Whoa. This one is often difficult to swallow. Most of us are taught early on that we can accomplish whatever we want to in life if we just work hard enough and put our minds to it. But as believers, we are called to depend on God.

Jesus' life on earth was lived in absolute dependence on God the Father. He said apart from the Father, He could do nothing. Let's take a look at one story from the Old Testament book of Joshua that illustrates the importance of following specific instructions when trying to defeat an enemy.

The Israelites walked in complete dependence on God as they circled Jericho seven times. With a trumpet blast and a loud shout, they then charged in and took the city.

If the people of Israel could march around Jericho seven times, surely, I can walk a journey of faith not knowing exactly how God will provide.

He Fights for You

"He jammed the wheels of their chariots so that they had diffi-culty driving. And the Egyptians said, "Let's get away from the Israelites! The LORD is fighting for them against Egypt." Exodus 14:25

I find this part of the Israelite's story intriguing. When God gave the word through Moses, the Israelites bolted from Egypt. It had been a long 430 years in captivity. After they left, Pharaoh had a change of heart and set out after his forced labor base.

At some point, however, they knew their battle was of a different nature. Even they knew the Israelite God was fighting for the Israelites and against the Egyptians.

We can approach the throne of grace with confidence because we have access to the One who can fight for us and we live in dependence on Him. Hebrews 4:16 tells us we can approach the throne of grace with confidence, so that we may receive mercy and find grace to help us in our time of need. We can come boldly before God's throne because of the name of Jesus.

A quote by Victor Hugo has ministered to me over the years. I can rest at night because God is by my side, and He fights for me.

> When you have laboriously completed your daily task, go to sleep in peace. We rest because he reigns. - Victor Hugo, French poet, novelist, essayist, playwright, and dramatist of the Romantic movement.

My friend, I pray that you can rest during this season you are experiencing right now. Let these ideas soak in. To the best of your ability, live a life of obedience, walk daily with God, and depend totally on Him.

Pray With Me

Lord, I want to be fueled by the power of Your Holy Spirit. Help me be obedient to Your Word and Your direction for my life. Help me to walk in your power today and depend on You completely. Thank you for keeping me on track and for fighting for me. Help me to say and do only those things that are pleasing to You. Your power within me is everything I need today. In Jesus' name, amen.

Questions for Reflection / Thoughts to Ponder

1. Think of a time when God specifically instructed you to act in a certain way. What did you do?

2. How can you keep your balance as you walk daily with God?

3. Think of a time when you experienced God's power and strength in your life. How did it affect you?

---

1. Mornings with Tozer 1991, 2008 Christian Publications

5

TRUST GOD'S LOVE

*Whoever dwells in the shelter of
the Most High will rest in the
shadow of the Almighty. I will say
of the Lord, "He is my refuge and
my fortress, my God, in whom I
trust." Psalm 91:1-2*

"I TRUST YOU"

About three weeks after my husband went to be with Jesus, the funeral home representative called letting me know the copies of his death certificate were ready to be picked up. I was headed to meet a friend for lunch, so I stopped there on my way to the restaurant.

While there, the rep asked if I wanted to take my husband's ashes with me as well. I had not even thought about that, but I said ok. When I got back in the car with the certificates in my lap and the box of ashes in the seat beside me, I completely lost it.

Later, I read the death certificate, which lists the cause of death. One thing led to another, but the first cause listed was diabetes. It rattled my brain. The doctors never said that diabetes was the cause. I began to question everything. Why hadn't I made the diabetic appointment with a specialist sooner? Had I missed any signs that he wasn't well?

Overcome with guilt, my anxiety that day rivaled any of the days in the hospital. I called my friend and pastor, needing to tell someone what I had learned. I'm sure he could hardly understand me with my emotions so out of control. Choked by sorrow, I asked the Lord "What am I going to do?"

And in my spirit, I clearly heard God say, "Are you going to trust me in this?" to which I immediately responded, "I don't know what else to do but to trust you."

Over the years, I've reminded myself of that moment with God. I've been tempted to take those words back — the decision to trust Him. To trust Him even when I didn't have all the answers. To trust no matter that the days ahead would be long and heartbreaking. To trust Him even though I didn't understand the why of it. Why God would take a godly man at the age of 45 who was husband and father to three sons?

I simply had to trust that God had a plan and remember that He loved me enough to send His Son to die for me. He settled His love right there, on the cross and anything else that happens, I can trust that He knows what's best.

I could say that I spent considerable effort guarding myself against allowing bitterness to become a stronghold in my life, but bitterness didn't present itself as an issue for me. As anyone else would do, I questioned God. But with three young boys, I was just trying to survive.

Oh, but this was so hard. It meant coming to the feet of Jesus every single day and saying, "I trust you."

These words in Proverbs were a balm to my soul.

Trust in the Lord with all your heart and lean not on your own understanding; in all your ways submit to him, and he will make your paths straight. Proverbs 3:5-6

Corrie Ten Boom, Holocaust survivor and Christian leader who became known for her teachings on forgiveness, is known to have said, "Never be afraid to trust an unknown future to a known God."

That is one of my favorite quotes. The thought helps me stay grounded when I begin to worry about what I should do or question how I could ever live without my husband. Especially during my boys' teenage years, oh how I've begun to question things! The teenage years can be stressful!

I don't claim to know all the answers, but I do know that I know my God. When I feel things are out of control, as they often seem, I know that God is still in control, and He is in control of my future. I must declare that His power strengthens me. His sovereignty allows things I can handle. His faithfulness sustains me.

When a negative thought comes to mind, we need to remember the truth of God's word. When Satan bombards us with accusations, we need to remember God's promises.

We must trust Him and not be afraid. God has not forgotten us. We can depend on Him to be our strength and our help when we're feeling overwhelmed, when fear holds us captive, guilt condemns us, or questions create doubts in our minds.

Our other option? We depend on ourselves or others. And this begs an honest answer to the question, "Can He meet my needs or not?"

Trust Conquers Guilt

Nearly two years after my husband's death, I was again gripped with guilt because of a conversation I had with a man I had just met during a work meeting.

I listened to him talk about how much his gastric bypass surgery had changed him. He decided to have the surgery because losing weight would help his sleep apnea.

He went on to say that this surgery had helped him with other diseases, like diabetes — that once you had the surgery, you no longer had diabetes. Thinking about it the rest of the afternoon, I wondered if that surgery would have made a difference for my husband. What if we had made that diabetes specialist appointment earlier and what if she had helped him before he collapsed?

Why couldn't my husband survive? We had so much left to do. He had so much still to contribute. I wanted to cry out to God again and beg for an answer.

The "what ifs" cripple us during any season of grief but especially when our loved one dies young. Those questions can be difficult to move past. But you can eventually move past them. A big part of gaining victory in this area is controlling what you allow your mind to think about.

I had not read my Bible that morning, so I sat on the porch swing that night to read. I read about Job and how he questioned God, and then read about God's responses.

I stopped when I reached this scripture.

"A person's days are determined; you have decreed the number of his months and have set limits he cannot exceed." Job 14:5

Wow. That was a hard one to wrap my head around. I believe that God showed me that nothing I or anyone could have done would have changed the outcome. Our God controls the universe and orders our lives. Our time here on Earth is in His hands.

The Lord helped me to accept this truth (again) and gave me the desire to live what's left of my life to the very fullest. He used that conversation followed by my personal search for answers, to remind me that He knows all and is in control of all. Our job? To trust His love.

Trust Beats Fear

"Don't hold on to the rocks when you're falling mommy. They will move. Trust me," my son Parker shouted to me in his deep raspy voice as we hiked up Pinnacle Mountain outside of Little Rock, Arkansas.

He was right. Those rocks would move.

Trust me. From the mouth of babes, right? According to my journal three years before my husband died, God had been speaking to me about just being with Him and trusting Him.

At that time, my boys' favorite Bible story was the one about David and Goliath. Typical boys — although they also loved the story about Leah — the girl no one loved.

Goliath was a nine-foot-tall giant, a champion among the Philistine army. He presented a bold proposal. If he fought against any Israelite soldier and won, the Israelites would serve the Philistines. If the Israelites won, the Philistines would serve the Israelites. The Israelites were terrified.

David arrived on the scene to check on his older brothers. David heard the story of Goliath's taunting and with confidence offered to fight the giant.

David asked the men standing near him, "What will be done for the man who kills this Philistine and removes this disgrace from Israel? Who is this uncircumcised Philistine that he should defy the armies of the living God?" 1 Samuel 17:26

I love that David defended his God. Oh, that I would fight my battles with such courage and confidence.

Saul tried to convince him he was not ready. But later, he prepared David with armor and weapons.

FACING THE GIANTS

I gave in to the begging for a puppy in 2022. I resisted at first because I knew it would be a lot of work and I didn't want more on my plate. However, I wanted my sons to be happy even more. But it definitely led me to question my sanity.

He was a little puppy with a big attitude. Our older dog was about 10 times his size. He must have looked like a giant in the puppy's eyes. You wouldn't have known it by the way he carried himself, strutting around like he owned the place. We soon realized we needed to start controlling this pup before he got too comfortable in his ways!

As children, we have the same attitude as this puppy, thinking we know it all until we grow up and realize just how much we don't know! But it's great to be so confident and courageous that we don't even realize we're facing a giant!

In the case of David and Goliath, I imagine that that was what David was like. He didn't even see the size of that giant - or the lion or bear he fought as a kid. He just saw the strength of his God. His plan was simple. He went to a stream and carefully selected five smooth stones. Then he got down to business.

Caleb didn't see the size of the giants when he explored the Promised Land either. Of course, he knew they were there, but he trusted God to do what He said He would do - that He would give them this land of milk and honey. His God had already demonstrated he could defeat the Egyptians. He could certainly defeat the Canaanites.

Caleb reported to the Israelites that with the Lord with them, they could take the land. He reminded them that God had promised it. His confidence is admirable. However, he and Joshua were shot down by the majority who did not have that same confidence in the Lord — they looked to their own weaknesses when considering whether to fight for the land, going so far as to threaten to kill them with stones. And the Israelites paid for their doubt and unbelief. It cost them 40 years of wandering in the wilderness. (Numbers 14:9, 14:24)

STEADFAST AND STRONG

Mary, the mother of Jesus, faced a different kind of giant than the Israelites. Her giant wasn't physical, but cultural. Mary didn't focus on the giant before her — being pregnant with the Lord out of wedlock. She was steadfast and strong, even at such a young age. She faced her giant with confidence and quiet strength. Plus, she demonstrated humility and the ability to worship. Her husband, Joseph, also did what was right and honorable.

Most of us will face a giant in our lives at one time or another. If you are a widow, the biggest giant of your life is likely the loss of your spouse. I believe there are moments in life when the simplest choice is the best choice, even when facing a giant.

What are some of your giants?

One of the first giants in my life was the loss of my first marriage where my dream of being a wife and mother came crashing down at the age of 25. I grieved that loss. Although it wasn't physical death, it was still a loss. I learned so much in the next few years. As I grieved, God comforted me. As I struggled with being alone, God was by my side. He taught me to forgive and healed me emotionally.

Then my family and I suffered the tragic loss of my nephew, Allen, when he was brutally beaten by his step-father at six years old. He was the only grandson/nephew in my family at the time. Talking with him on the phone on Christmas Day three months before his death, something didn't feel right. He lived in another town so we prayed that God would take care of him for us. God did take care of him. He took him out of an abusive situation and brought him home to Him.

After two miscarriages, my husband and I lost our infant daughter, Ashlynn. We had learned at 20 weeks our baby had zero chance of survival once she was born. I knew God could change our situation if He wanted to. However, I never got a sense that He would do so. That long, dark and lonely road brought many tears, but in it, we also found encouragement and blessing along the way.

Following that, I lost my best friend, Angie, after a five-year battle with cancer. She was 44.

And then of course the loss of my precious lifelong friend and husband, Matthew. Nothing prepared me for the ache in my heart as I said goodbye to him.

Through the different seasons of grief in my life, I can confidently say God has shown himself faithful.

Scripture tells us that we will overcome our trials.

"Not by might, nor by my power, but by my spirit says the LORD of hosts." Zechariah 4:6 (ESV)

May God help us to walk and operate with help from God's spirit and not do things by our own strength. He is the maker of heaven and earth. Surely, we can trust him for the help we need.

FACING THE BATTLE

David and Goliath both took different approaches when it came to the battle.

Goliath suited up in heavy armor, including carrying a shield bearer and a spear. David picked five stones and a slingshot.

My response when facing a battle has been less than stellar or commendable at times. I often retreat to avoid getting hurt or talk to friends instead of the Lord. I try to figure things out on my own. And of course, many times my giants aren't really giants at all. I blow things all out of proportion and in hindsight, they seem small. It's easy to lose perspective.

David confronted the enemy with confidence in his God. He kept his eyes on the Lord. His wasn't an emergency kind of faith. God was his guide day in and day out. Trust was as natural to him as taking his next breath.

David said to the Philistine, "You come against me with sword and spear and javelin, but I come against you in the name of the Lord Almighty, the God of the armies of Israel, whom you have defied. This day the Lord will deliver you into my hands, and I'll strike you down and cut off your head. This very day I will give the carcasses of the Philistine army to the birds and the wild animals, and the whole world will know that there is a God in Israel. All those gathered here will know that it is not by sword or spear that the Lord saves; for the battle is the Lord's, and he will give all of you into our hands." 1 Samuel 17: 45-47

As this passage so clearly conveys, God is the source of victory in our lives. Over the years, I have learned that without Christ, I can do nothing. Christ alone can calm the raging sea.

Certainly, the story about Goliath shows us that it wasn't about power and strength. It's not the physical armor we place around us that keeps us from getting hurt. It's who we know. David knew the One who has all authority in heaven and on earth.

God tells us to remain faithful to Him. Always. He died to save us from sin, doubt and worry. Trusting Him means leaving fear and the uncertainties of our lives behind and placing our trust in Christ alone. When we do, He promises to give us peace beyond our understanding.

As the song *In Christ Alone* by Michael English tells us, we are to place our trust in Christ alone. I have known this song most of my adult life. The song reminds us that though we could take pride in our own accomplishments, we will glory in Him alone. We overcome through His strength. It is through putting our faith in Christ that we find strength and hope.

Trust Reveals God's Faithfulness

Looking back, the years without my husband have been a blip in time and yet also feel like an eternity. I have seen sorrow and pain, but also comfort. My family has experienced times when we were at our worst, but also times of joy. Tears, but also laughter. Failures, yet accomplishments, too. Fear and anxiety but also confidence. After seven years, I still miss my husband every day, but am grateful for the years we had together and the confidence that one day we will see him again.

Through it all, God has been faithful.

If you have lost a spouse or experienced any kind of major trauma in your life, I encourage you to try to bring good from it. Often our misery becomes our ministry. In each instance of the giants I shared, God has placed me in situations where my experience, and God's work in my life, could encourage someone else as they walk a similar journey.

LOOK FORWARD IN FAITH

I have found the words of Matt Redman's song *Never Once* to be true today and for the days to come. I took comfort in the words that spoke of God's faithfulness. Through it all, I never walked alone. God never left me on my own. He is faithful.

No matter what difficult circumstances, situations, or giants face us today, we can trust His love for us. We can take our eyes off our situation and look to the faithfulness of God. That doesn't mean we will always understand why He has allowed hardships and trials in our life. But He has given us examples through scripture and in our own lives that give us confidence that He cares for us.

Even though mankind fell in the Garden of Eden, allowing sickness, disease and many evils into the world, God in His mercy made a way for us to be with Him one day in a perfect world.

Our creator, the Almighty God, our rescuer, our fortress, redeemer, protector, comforter, savior, and king is praiseworthy. If God is the maker of heaven and earth and all that is in it, then we can trust Him.

Contemporary Christian music singer and songwriter Lauren Daigle's song *Trust in You* sums up this chapter about trusting God's love. Sometimes God doesn't move the mountain we want Him to move. Sometimes He doesn't part the waters so we can walk through safely. Sometimes He doesn't give the answers we want. But His ways are higher, and His plans are good. We can trust Him to be our strength and our comfort.

We can trust God's love.

Pray With Me

Lord, I trust in Your love. Help me to fight my battles with courage and confidence. Please give me wisdom for today, and help me not to regret or worry about what happened yesterday, or what is to come tomorrow. Even when I don't understand why things happen, I can rest in the fact that everything is made under your rule and governance. Be my life. Be my breath. Be my guide day in and day out. Help me to put complete trust in You. In Jesus' name, amen.

————————————— 🎩 —————————————

I lift up my eyes to the mountains — where does my help come from? My help comes from you, Lord, the maker of heaven and earth. Psalm 121:1-2

Do not fear, for I have redeemed you; I have summoned you by name; you are mine. When you pass through the waters, I will be with you; and when you pass through the rivers, they will not sweep over you. When you walk through the fire, you will not be burned; the flames will not set you ablaze. For I am the Lord your God, the Holy One of Israel, your Savior. Isaiah 43:1-3

And may you have the power to understand, as all God's people should, how wide, how long, how high, and how deep his love is. May you experience the love of Christ, though it is too great to understand fully. Then you will be made complete with all the fullness of life and power that comes from God. Ephesians 3:18-19 (NLT)

Questions for Reflection / Thoughts to Ponder

1. Name some of your giants. What is your approach when it comes to battling those giants?

2. God has a plan and we can trust that He knows what's best. Write out your deepest struggles about trusting His plan.

3. Think of David. How can we live in that same confidence and trust in God's love?

Part 2

Find Blessing in the Pain

6

PRAISE CHANGES THINGS

My tongue will proclaim your
righteousness, your praises all day
long. Psalm 35:28

I once heard someone say that when you look for God's blessings, you
will find them. I will be the first to admit that the experience of losing
my husband didn't automatically bring praise to my lips or the feeling
of being blessed to my mind. But I distinctly remember talking to God
while at my husband's hospital bedside.

Matthew rarely sat still. Even when on a phone call, he paced the floor,
whether at work or at home. Seeing him in a hospital bed with wires
and tubes was almost more than I could bear. They put him through
a procedure where they wrapped his body in a cooling blanket. The
process cooled down his body, then slowly began warming it back up
again.

As much as I prayed and pleaded with God, there was a point over
those five days that I was willing to accept whatever was to come. At that
time, I told Matthew I loved him and that it was okay if he had to go.

There were many times over those first few days I begged my husband to hang in there, that we all needed him. Those days left my soul dry, my spirit broken. But at some point, I knew I had to let go and I gave him permission as well.

I cried out to my God to heal Matthew but decided in my heart that if He didn't, I would still praise Him. I believe it is important to accept that God knows why things happen, even when we don't understand.

He is worthy of all our praise, in times of joy and times of grief. He is worthy even through whatever circumstance, trial, or pain wrecks our world. He never promised us a perfect life on earth, only a perfect eternity for those who know Him.

Praise the Lord. Praise the Lord, my soul. I will praise the Lord all my life; I will sing praise to my God as long as I live. Psalm 146:1-2

He is the Maker of heaven and earth, the sea, and everything in them — the LORD, he remains faithful forever. Psalm 146:6

Praise Him When Circumstances Cloud the Truth

I remember my aunt and uncle singing the song *Excuses* (by the Kingsmen) in church and it makes me smile.

The song tells of the devil's scheme to give us excuses that will keep us away from church. He knows that when people come to the Lord, he loses, so he offers us excuses.

Another version of that song could be Choices. I choose to believe that God's Word is true. I choose to praise Him in the storm. I choose to obey His word, to accept His will. Satan would have us choose anything that would distract our devotion to God.

We see many examples in the Bible of those who chose to praise God despite difficult circumstances.

Hunted down by Saul, David chose to praise the Lord. While running for his life, David cried out to God.

I love you, O LORD, my strength. The LORD is my rock, my fortress and my deliverer; my God is my rock, in whom I take refuge, He is my shield and the horn of my salvation, my strong-hold. Psalm 18:1-2

In his despair, Job chose to praise the Lord. He did not sin despite his circumstances.

At this, Job got up and tore his robe and shaved his head. Then he fell to the ground in worship and said: Naked I came from my mother's womb, and naked I will depart. The Lord gave and the Lord has taken away; may the name of the Lord be praised. Job 1:20-22

In her great anguish and grief, Hannah poured out her soul to the Lord. After that, she went out with joy. The next day, she worshipped the Lord and went home.

Or our choices could go another, more dangerous way. I could choose to believe the lies of Satan. I could choose to believe God doesn't care, that He's not really there for me.

We must remind ourselves of the voice of truth. Peter tells us that the eyes of the Lord are on the righteous and his ears are attentive to their prayers (1 Peter 3:12). We may not always feel this way, but this is truth. He is attentive to our prayers.

Another truth is that some days — even a lot of days — can be good. And in time, we can learn to accept the good days at face value and appreciate them when they come. Not that we'd ever be okay with what happened to our spouse, but eventually we can accept it and continue to live. We can go on to thrive and not just survive.

I remember the day my oldest son, Connor, became an Eagle Scout, and then later the day we celebrated with friends and family in the formal ceremony. His dad had been his biggest encourager and supporter throughout scouting. The accomplishment honored his dad and reminded the family of many special memories. After Connor handed out his mentor pins, there wasn't a dry eye in the place. Days like those warm our hearts.

Although the memory of the pain we went through may stay for a while, the pain will eventually lessen. Scripture is full of verses that tell us to give thanks in all circumstances, avoid complaining, and pray continually. We must make a conscious decision of the will to obey God in these areas.

Truth is, giving thanks *in all circumstances* is the will of God. Let us turn away from the lies Satan places before us and choose to listen to the voice of truth.

Praise Him When Storms Threaten

The first winter after my husband's passing, I wanted to give my boys a trip that would be fun and memorable. I tried to keep our lives as normal as possible for our family, even though the family unit didn't come close to resembling what we once had. My husband had always made our trips so fun, and I wanted to carry on the tradition. I loved snow skiing and decided that was just the adventure the boys and I needed. They were 13, 10, and 8.

I booked a last-minute condo — well it wasn't even a condo. It was a small motel about 20 minutes from a ski resort in New Mexico. We traveled from our home in Louisiana to New Mexico with a stop in Oklahoma City to visit family for the holidays.

The night before leaving Oklahoma City, warnings of an oncoming blizzard on our route led me to doubt my decision. I discussed with my family whether I should wait it out. Waiting it out would mean delaying our trip by one day and I didn't want to wait. I plowed ahead into what was only sleet when we first left. That quickly changed.

It was an adventure alright. Somewhere east of Amarillo, Texas, this Louisiana girl drove through white-out conditions. This meant that with the sky being overcast from blowing snow and the ground covered with snow, the landscape appeared entirely white, and we were unable to see the horizon.

I assigned my 13-year-old, in the front passenger seat, to look out the window and follow the boundary line on the road, while I had my eyes glued on the center line. Stopping on the side of the road during a whiteout was not an option.

The two younger boys in the backseat were bug-eyed and terrified. I lost control twice, sliding into the median, but somehow steered the car back onto the road. I did some serious praying that day and we finally drove out of the storm outside of Amarillo. They don't teach that type of defensive driving in Louisiana!

That day I learned that the Lord protects us even when we make stupid decisions. We were literally carried through the storm.

Recovering from the loss of a loved one also takes us through an emotional storm. They may not be physical ice or snowstorms, but they are storms, all the same, that sap our strength and weary our souls. God help us as we try to navigate them! And He always does.

Jesus Calms Our Storms

The disciples faced their own storm in a boat while Jesus was sleeping. While He napped, a storm began to brew. Not just any storm, but a storm of white-out proportions. The disciples were terrified for their lives, doing whatever they could physically do to survive. But the master of the storm slept soundly at the back of the boat. Awakened by the disciples, He calmed the sea in just three words — Quiet! Be still!

According to Mark, Jesus got up, rebuked the wind and said to the waves, "Quiet! Be still!" Then the wind died down and it was completely calm. Mark 4:39

Battered by the storm, there wasn't much they could do but call out to Jesus. Terrified in a different way, they asked this question.

"Who is this? Even the wind and the waves obey him!" Mark 4:41

This verse has always left me in awe. This was the moment the disciples recognized the power Jesus possessed — the very wind obeyed His command!

My boys and I survived the storm that day, but did I ever question my ability to care for them on my own! I'm sure the disciples questioned their own ability to survive the storm, too. They went from "Teacher, don't you care if we drown?" to being in awe at the power of the man who could calm the raging sea.

God had bigger plans for them that day. And He has plans for us too. Sometimes we just need a "Quiet, Be still" moment to recognize God's power.

The song *Praise You In This Storm*, by Casting Crowns has special meaning for me. It's a song we like to sing along to, until it becomes real. Do we really want to praise God through the storm? Or do we just want deliverance from it? Most likely, we just want to avoid the storm altogether.

The song reassures us that God is with us even though rain may describe our lives. It encourages us to praise God even through the storms of our lives.

Praise Him When Memories Pierce Our Hearts

I think hitting that one-year anniversary of a loved one's death is a monumental milestone. It doesn't miraculously make the pain go away, but at that point, you've passed all the first holidays, birthdays, and anniversaries.

There was a time during that first year when I felt I missed my husband more with each passing day. As a matter of fact, I wrote that in my journal. I would re-read posts written about him on social media. Memories popped up on Facebook, reminding me of our times together.

Oh how people loved and appreciated him. Not as much as me though. How I wish I could have had one more day to be with him and show him in person.

We face daily reminders of how things used to be, of the family we had been before. We often refer to the timing of events as either before his death or after. Milestones with the kids, anniversaries, birthdays. . . Sometimes I felt it would have been easier to avoid them than to face the pain they caused. But to do that would mean missing out on the joy those memories can also bring.

My husband's absence during the Christmas season was one of the hardest adjustments for our family. He loved the holiday and loved gathering our friends and family around us. Our annual Christmas party for adults and children was the highlight for us, and many of our friends as well. After a discussion with my sons, we decided to keep the tradition. Yes, there is still a sting of pain without him, but they also hold many fond memories for our family.

Even If

The first time I heard Mercy Me's song *Even If*, I was a mess. It was *my* song. I had prayed. Many had prayed. But God did not move that mountain. And I had said if He didn't, I would still praise Him. This song captured my thoughts exactly and still does.

I knew God was able. I knew God could make the sorrow go away. And like the song vocalizes, I knew my only hope was in Him.

Don't miss that. *Our hope is in God alone.* The words of that song pierced my heart. Oh, to live where our hope is Christ alone. On January 1, 2015, I wrote in my journal that I prayed the year would bring a new start, a refreshing time for my family. I asked God to bless that year. Nine months later, my husband was gone.

Feelings of helplessness and hopelessness set in. As I experienced emptiness and pain, I sought God's strength and power, asking Him to surround us with His love. A year later, it still seemed like yesterday and sometimes still does today. At that time, I wrote I would praise Him through this storm in my journal. A simple statement, but one that's easier said than done.

Praise Him Before the Stones Do

Toward the end of Jesus' ministry, He makes His triumphant entry into Jerusalem. The people begin praising God for all the miracles they had seen Him perform. The Pharisees didn't like it and told Jesus to rebuke them. Jesus' response? He told the Pharisees if they were silent, the very stones would cry out.

"I tell you," he replied, "if they keep quiet, the stones will cry out."
Luke 19:40

Before my husband's death, and even afterward, my car was the place for our "little boy" spiritual conversations. Talking with three boys about God can sometimes be entertaining . . . and challenging. One night on the way home from my women's Bible study group meeting, we began talking about praising God and specifically, what happens when we don't praise God. So I told them that the Bible says if we are silent, even the rocks and trees will praise Him.

Parker, who was four at the time, proceeded to tell me emphatically "I'm not going to praise Him. I'm not going to praise Him." I asked him why and he answered, "I want to see that! I want to see the trees praise Him!"

Thinking for a moment, I came up with this response. "Look at the trees, how their branches are all pointing up. See, they're praising God. Their branches are lifted up toward heaven." That satisfied him for a time. For a while, he would occasionally ask me, "Mom, is that tree praising God?"

God will be praised. If not from our lips, then from the rocks and trees.

The fact that God uses my children to focus my heart and soul on something leaves me in awe. Before the rocks cry out or the trees shout, I will praise the Lord. When I'm having a good day, I will praise Him. When I'm in the middle of a storm, I will praise Him.

From the rising of the sun to the place where it sets, the name of the LORD is to be praised. Psalm 113:3

Pray With Me

Lord, You know that life can be painful. You lived it. Yet you honored Your Father through it all. You have heard the cries of my heart and I thank you for Your strength and comfort. I want to honor You and give thanks through all of my circumstances. I pray that You will hear my heart, and receive my praise. Help me to be strong and courageous in the midst of life's storms. Your strength is all I need. In Jesus' name, amen.

———————————— 🎩 ————————————

O Lord, I will honor and praise your name, for you are my God. You do such wonderful things! Isaiah 25:1 (NLT)

All your works praise you, Lord; your faithful people extol you. Psalm 145:10

Let the trees of the forest sing, let them sing for joy before the LORD, for he comes to judge the earth. 1 Chronicles 16:33

Let the rivers clap their hands, let the mountains sing together for joy. Psalm 98:8

———————————— 🎩 ————————————

Questions for Reflection / Thoughts to Ponder

1. Think of a time when you have listened to the lies of Satan over

the Voice of Truth from the Scriptures. How has God proven He is attentive to your prayers?

2. How difficult is it for you to praise Him in the storms of your life? What hinders you the most?

3. Has there been a time when you were able to praise God through your loss? How did that impact your life? What helped you focus on praising God? What would you do differently?

7

REMEMBER TO REMEMBER

I will remember the deeds of
the Lord; yes, I will remember
your wonders of old. Psalm 77:11
(ESV)

I believe memories play a part in our journey to healing. Our memories can help us process our loss. Although they are not here physically, we can still connect to our loved ones emotionally through our memories.

Some of the things we have done as a family reflect on events and times we shared with my husband. I encouraged our boys to talk about him from the beginning. It soon became second nature to mention him in our conversations.

We remember things my husband said, his favorite songs and food, and his common sayings. We talk about what he would have thought about something we were doing. Recalling and reflecting on our favorite memories inspires us to focus on the good things in our lives.

Not only remember the good and sad moments but also remember God's blessing during your grief. In order to keep your perspective, it can be helpful to keep a journal recording other circumstances from which God has already delivered you.

Keep a Reminder

In the old hymn *Come Thou Fount,* the writer says he raises his Ebenezer.

Here I raise my Ebenezer
Here by Thy great help I've come
And I hope by Thy good pleasure
Safely to arrive at home

What does it mean to raise our Ebenezer? The Hebrew meaning of the name Ebenezer is "stone of help," which references 1 Samuel 7:12.

While under attack from the Philistines, the Israelites begged Samuel, a prophet of the Lord, to cry out to the Lord to rescue them. Samuel did, offering a sacrifice and prayer for God's deliverance.

According to 1 Samuel 7:12, Samuel took a stone and set it between the two cities of Mizpah and Shen, naming the stone Ebenezer, saying "Thus far the Lord has helped us."

This stone reminded the Israelites to remember what the Lord had done for them. Even future generations would see it and be reminded of how God showed them grace and mercy in their time of great need.

THE CHAIR

I have a leather chair in my living room where I sit for my morning devotions. Paired with just the right blanket, it's warm and inviting. Big and comfy with an ottoman for stretching out, this chair bids me stop and rest for a while.

As I sat one morning, memories filled my mind. Matthew sitting in it after a day at work, sometimes falling asleep. Matthew reading a book to the boys as they sat on its arms and gathered around him. Christmas morning, it is "the place" for Santa's delivery of goods for one of the boys. My father-in-law taking an afternoon nap in it after Christmas lunch. During my ladies' Bible study, one friend always claims it as hers.

Sometimes leaving the comfort of that chair takes effort. It's like an old friend that beckons me to sit and stay for a while.

It seems odd to say it, but I am blessed by that chair. Blessed because it holds memory after memory for me — all pointing to God's blessing and goodness. The more time I spend seeking God in that quiet spot, the more blessings He brings to my mind. I believe remembering God's blessings on our lives helps us look beyond the pain of the moment to dwell on the good and pleasing things in life.

Remember the wonders he has done, his miracles, and the judgments he pronounced. 1 Chronicles 16:12

WAY TO GO!

The second time I visited Savannah, Georgia was in 2017. I planned to run a half marathon, but my heart really wasn't in it. As I began to prepare physically and mentally for the day, Facebook reminded me that my first time in the city was five years prior when I ran my first marathon with my friend Angela.

It was my sweet husband who posted that achievement saying, "way to go!!" Oh, how I miss him! He was always in my corner, proud of me. He didn't always say the words, but he showed it through his actions. As a matter of fact, I often found out through other people how proud he was of my accomplishments.

I miss the way he laughed at me and called me Trisha. I miss the way he would talk me into singing with him in the car on road trips. I miss the way he paced the room when we were talking or when he was on the phone. I miss the way he sat and read to the boys. I miss the way he held my hand. I miss the loud sound machine he used every night to help him sleep and how he had to sleep with the room completely dark.

I miss the way he laughed out loud. I miss seeing him look at his iPad in the evenings, flipping through news and pictures. I miss hearing him play loud music from his home office and how he would sometimes work at the kitchen counter. I miss how he would make sure everything was in its place and organized. I miss our bike rides and our Sunday naps.

I even miss the annoying way he pointed out when I had a rogue hair on my chin. I mean, who's going to tell me that now? I fear my boys just might blurt it out to me in front of a crowd!

I miss how he was fiercely protective and how he had to know where I was and that I was always safe. I miss how he wanted me to just sit and be with him while he hung out in his home office. I miss how he pushed me to be my very best.

My prayer and question that day in Savannah and many times since was, "would the pain inside of my chest ever go away?" Sometimes it felt too much to carry. Plus there were responsibilities and activities to attend to. I prayed that day that I would do well, that I would do something to make the Lord proud and make Matthew proud too.

I want to encourage those of you who are still in the stages of intense grief, that the sting of pain will ease over time. While my boys and I will always miss Matthew's physical presence, we can still celebrate his life and legacy.

Today I pray that as you navigate the loneliness, the questions, and a host of seesaw emotions, you would have the strength to press on and accomplish what God has called you to do. That call could simply be taking care of the basic needs of your family, excelling in your job, or helping others. Your life still counts. While some are held captive by their sorrow, Jesus came so that you could live your life to the full.

Keep Your Perspective

Remembering what the Lord has done for us — and others — helps us keep perspective when we are recovering from great loss or hit with any kind of significant trial. The prophet Micah reminds us to remember the acts of the Lord. He also foretold of the birth of Christ in Bethlehem and reminds us that God is ready and waiting to forgive and restore those who repent.

"Remember your journey from Shittim to Gilgal, that you may know the righteous acts of the Lord." Micah 6:5

When we are down, remembering the good things God has done may just be the thing to move us forward in our journey.

Before my husband walked out of our bedroom that fateful September morning, he told me he loved me. Those were the last words he ever spoke to me. Not only will I remember that moment for the rest of my days, but I have also recalled many, many moments when he expressed his love for our boys and me.

- He sat down the afternoon before the day he collapsed and drew cover pages for two of our boys' school binders.

- He encouraged me to train for and run marathons.

- He valued family and gathered our families together countless times for special occasions and holidays.

- He loved bringing people together and welcoming people to our home. More was always better. He was a "more the merrier" kind of guy.

- He bought and sent me a fluffy robe from a hotel where he stayed on a business trip, just because.

These memories are sweet companions. However, remembering them can cause fresh pain, and avoiding them is often easier than facing the pain. But when we do that, we miss out on the joy those memories can also bring.

When we feel like the enemy is closing in and only a miracle can save us, we need to remember our Ebenezer. We need to remember those times that we prayed for help in a difficult situation, for restored health, or for a relationship to be reconciled and God provided. Once we're past that emergency time in our lives, we need to remember His provision. When we do, we have renewed strength to endure the struggle of our current trial.

A Matter of Perspective

Sitting in my favorite chair one spring morning, I began to think about and look forward to my day. In less than a minute, I went from feeling lighthearted and excited about the day and looking forward to what God had in store for me, to a deep-rooted ache in my heart, remembering my loss. How does that even happen? I am convinced that memories are good for the soul, but do they tend to turn into grief all over again?

When we're grief stricken, we need to condition our minds to keep our perspective and focus on the good things God has done. That can be a spiritual battle, literally. Be patient and understanding with yourself.

God's perspective is more about the longer term and healing. He chooses to bless us through our memories if we let Him. The Apostle Paul tells us if anything is excellent or praiseworthy, think about such things (Philippians 4:8).

Our memories play an important role in our journey. Even remembering the good days can help us get through our not-so-good days.

As my boys and I left the mountains to finish up their first ski trip in 2015, a memory popped into my mind. Early in our marriage, Matthew and I took a ski trip with a group of friends. First, let me say that scheduling a ski trip during the busiest time of the year for my job wasn't the smartest idea. But when you live in the South, you've got to go where the snow is when you can. The night before the trip, I stayed at work to re-work parts of the annual report before production and ended up working through the night. So my husband packed for both of us. As a matter of fact, he and our friends went on to Dallas without me and I hitched a ride on the company plane and met them there before flying to the mountains.

You may have guessed this story ends with a wardrobe disaster. When we got to the mountains, I learned that he had decided to pack light and brought a couple of sweaters that we could share. He'd wear one on one day, I'd wear it the next. I was not thrilled with that scenario, and I believe that was the last time he packed for me! His perspective and mine were quite different. Oh, but what a fun memory.

Bob Dylan, American singer-songwriter, once said, "Take care of all your memories. For you cannot relive them."

Our memories help us heal, so I encourage you to hold them tightly. Write about them. Write about the big events. Write about the little things. Write what makes you cry. Write what makes you laugh. As time goes on, even the painful ones will bring a smile.

Keep a Journal of What God has Already Said

There may be times when we sit in silence, and it seems we are all alone. That's when we need to remember when God spoke to us before. Keep a journal of what He's already said to you. Sometimes in my quiet time, certain verses will jump out at me. So I write them down and have been blessed by doing so. When I write them, I spend more time with them, and my faith grows.

- Writing out scripture makes me slow down and focus on its meaning.

- Writing out scripture helps me go deeper with God and apply those truths to my life.

- Writing out scripture helps my wandering mind understand and retain what I've read.

- Writing out scripture leaves a tangible source of encouragement for later on.

Remembering what God has already said encourages and energizes us to keep moving forward.

Even the two disciples on the road to Emmaus comforted themselves when they realized they had been in the presence of Jesus and remembered what He had said. Luke 24:32 tells us "Were not our hearts burning within us while he talked with us on the road and opened the scriptures to us?"

And then later in the upper room, the two disciples told the eleven and those with them what happened.

Then the two told what had happened on the way, and how Jesus was recognized by them when he broke the bread. Luke 24:35

Although things may look hopeless in the moment, we need to look no further than scripture to understand — as these disciples did — what happened and what will happen. First, Christ had to suffer and *then* be glorified.

According to Luke's gospel, the women intent on tending to Jesus' body in the tomb were also reminded to remember what Jesus said.

As they came to place spices on His body, they were confronted with an empty tomb. While they wondered what had happened, two men whose clothes gleamed like lightning spoke to them.

"Why do you look for the living among the dead? He is not here; he has risen! Remember how he told you, while he was still with you?" Luke 24:5-6

Why were the women surprised? Hadn't he told them He would rise again? If so, why should we wonder if Jesus is with us? If our faith is in Jesus Christ, we already have what we need.

After the angels reminded them of Jesus' words, the women remembered what he had said. (Luke 24:8) Jesus had told them that he would suffer, be killed, and on the third day be raised to life.

In our darkest moments, we need to remember the things He has already told us, the things He has already done for us. This keeps His faithfulness in the forefront of our minds.

Even when we hear no voice, we can be encouraged through the knowledge of what the Lord has already said and done. Abide in that knowledge.

I encourage you to take a moment and listen to Steven Curtis Chapman's song *Remember to Remember*, which speaks to the Christian from God's perspective and describes where He carried the believer along the journey. God guides us through the mountains and valleys of our lives. Even though the way may be dark, He promises to be there with us. When we look back — when we remember — where we've been and God's hand in that, we can move forward.

Keep Memories Alive

Our lives changed forever after my husband passed away, but our memories helped us through each milestone and significant event for our family. I have tried to keep my husband's memory alive as we have walked this journey. And many others also provided ways to memorialize his death and his gift of organ donation.

Here are a few examples of meaningful activities that our family does/did to preserve Matthew's memory.

- I started a book for friends and family to write their favorite memories of Matthew. I've taped letters from people who mailed or emailed me notes about him and included some of my own sweet memories.

- Photos of him with us fill our home, telling our family story.

- I created a memory book with photos of my husband with each son and gave it to them one Christmas.

- I created Facebook posts on special occasions.

- I regularly remind my boys of Matthew's favorite sayings and favorite songs when they come on the radio.

- I talk to my sons about their dad often, what he would say and do in certain situations, and speak with them about significant events in his life.

- We tell stories. My sons have told me my husband let them drink a sip of beer once. I am still not convinced that is true!

- We also take intentional steps to remember.

  - We hosted a bike ride with our church community and friends on the one-year anniversary of his death.

  - We have released balloons in our backyard on several of his birthdays.

  - We have taken bike rides on many Father's Days (because that was one of his favorite things to do).

We never stop missing him, but we have learned to move forward with hope, healing, and peace within our memories.

As memories surface, triggered by a familiar place, a favorite phrase, or even the smell of his cologne, take a moment to remember, reflect and heal.

Remember to Remember

How God-honoring would it be if we were in the habit of raising our own Ebenezers — our own stones of remembrance — to allow us to see God's hand in our past and give us the assurance and faith that He will provide for us in the future?

God is the wellspring of every blessing in our lives. When He does something good in your life, acknowledge it. Write it down. Tell someone. Your testimony of God's goodness can be a way to overcome the enemy. If you're on social media, make a post of gratitude. It will come back to you as a reminder in the future.

We also need to remember the things God has already told us. His faithfulness has been proven over and over through his Word.

Remembering the good things God has done and the promises He has made, even in the middle of trial and grief, may just be the thing to help us move forward in our journey.

Pray With Me

Jesus, help me to *remember to remember*. You are a good, good God and Your Word reminds me of that every day. Thank You for carrying me through the most difficult points in my life and the promise that You are there for every step in my journey. Thank You for helping me keep things in perspective. Help me to walk through life with a new set of eyes that are focused on You, and to live from Your eternal perspective. In Jesus' name, amen.

Questions for Reflection / Thoughts to Ponder

1. Memories can be oh so painful. Write down those that are the most difficult for you. Write down how they make you feel. Think about how God has also brought blessings from them.

2. We need to keep our perspective and focus on the good things God has done. What memories or blessings bring you the most comfort?

3. Think about how you can raise your own Ebenezer. What stones of remembrance would you place there?

8

GRATITUDE CHANGES OUR ATTITUDE

*The Lord is my strength and my
shield; In him my heart trusts,
and I am helped; My heart exults,
and with my song I give thanks to
him. Psalm 28:7 (ESV)*

There are images forever etched in my memory. The drive to the hospital. Watching hospital personnel unload Matthew from the ambulance. Once so full of life and energy, my husband lying completely still in the hospital bed. My three boys sitting on the couch as I explained the grim situation, but that we should still pray — believing — for God to heal. None of these images foster an attitude of gratitude.

However, through it all, God showed me that there were parts of the experience that called for gratitude. He gave me the ability to recognize His hand at work. I could also be thankful because of who God is as well as the peace He gives in tragic situations. He gave me good days. And even in raw pain, I could still live my life and love the people right in front of me.

THE WHIRLWIND OF HEAVEN

What an astonishing story when Elijah is taken up to Heaven in a whirlwind. (2 Kings 2:1-15) Just the sight of it must have been breathtaking.

Elijah and Elisha were two of the most well-known prophets of Israel. They both served in the northern kingdom of Israel. God had told Elijah, the elder of the two, to anoint Elisha as a prophet.

One day, Elijah gave Elisha a "heads up" that the Lord was going to take him (Elijah). Elisha wasn't ready for Elijah to leave and said as much. As the two were walking and talking together, God picked Elijah up in a chariot. I'm trying to picture that scene. To have seen Elisha's reaction when that chariot arrived! Did Elijah just step into it and then the whirlwind whisked him away?

As they were walking along and talking together, suddenly a chariot of fire and horses of fire appeared and separated the two of them, and Elijah went up to heaven in a whirlwind. Elisha saw this and cried out, "My father! My father! The chariots and horsemen of Israel!" And Elisha saw him no more. Then he took hold of his garment and tore it in two. Elisha then picked up Elijah's cloak that had fallen from him and went back and stood on the bank of the Jordan. He took the cloak that had fallen from Elijah and struck the water with it. "Where now is the Lord, the God of Elijah?" he asked. 2 Kings 2:11-14

Rich Mullins wrote a song about it. Rich went out exactly the way he describes in his song *"Elijah."* Rich's song indicated he wanted to leave like Elijah — a whirlwind to fuel his chariot of fire. His chariot was his Jeep and He died instantly in an accident.

I played this song at my husband's memorial service because that was the way he would have wanted to go and what essentially happened. He never recovered from the moment he collapsed. The doctor said he never knew what hit him, which was of some comfort to me. They certainly tried everything they could to give us some hope . . . or maybe it was to alleviate any hope. But in the end, he left us too soon at only 45 years old.

Be Thankful for God's Hand at Work

As difficult as that time was, I could see God's hand in the many things that happened that week. I was grateful that:

- My husband didn't suffer. He rode his bike to the track. When he met his buddies there, he told them he felt great. He was enjoying the morning one moment and enjoying the presence of Jesus the next.

- I didn't have to make a decision about life support. After his collapse on the track, he spent five days undergoing multiple tests and procedures. The bottom line — there was no brain activity. When that is the case, the doctor simply declares a brain death. I remember praying that God would make the decision for me because I could not if it came to that. And God, in His mercy, answered.

- My husband clearly made known his preference to not allow people to see him once he was gone. I'm pretty sure I knew that after only a couple of dates with him. He dreaded funerals and certainly never wanted to see an open casket. During his hospital stay, people close to him were able to say goodbye, while honoring his wish. I trusted that was an answer to prayer as well. God protected me from the anxiety of that decision.

- I struggled with the decision to let our boys see him in that unconscious state. At 13, 10, and 8 years of age, the hospital intensive care environment can be very intimidating with all its machines and wires. But I'm grateful I did because they were able to have that last time to see him and talk to him.

- Not able to sleep or rest the evening before we were to learn the final test results that would determine brain activity, I went back to the hospital in the middle of the night just to be with him. I sat and held his hand all night.

The next morning we were told there was no response at all. It was what they had led us to expect, but oh how I still hoped that we would see a miracle that day.

Our boys had asked me what the doctors were saying. I told them that they did not give us much hope, but that we should still pray, and believe he would get better. It was so hard to know the right words and I'm still not sure if I handled it the best way. They still expected him to recover so the news was a blow and shock.

It didn't seem real. My husband, the one who kept our family laughing, always the life of the party, quick-witted, creative and generous, was gone

God blessed me with my in-law's love and acceptance. Syd and Sara Cameron did well raising their son. His brother and sister and nieces and their families have also been a continued blessing in our lives. I am grateful for my own family who also stepped up to meet specific needs in the trying days that followed.

I am grateful because Jesus was with me from the moment my friends knocked on the door of my home that first morning until the time we walked out of his memorial service. The Lord was there in the months of adjusting and the years of longing and remembering. He was there in my time of need and when I felt attacked by Satan. His presence is still with me today.

He is there for you too. I am not suggesting we are to be thankful for our trials, although James 1:1 tells us to consider them joy because they produce perseverance. I do not believe God is asking us to be thankful that we lost our spouse or for the hardships we've had to endure.

I am certainly not suggesting we fake how we feel. My hope is that we can be real with ourselves and others. It's about being grateful for the time we had with our spouse and the memories we cherish. Remember our hope comes from a relationship with Jesus Christ. Being authentic and real with our feelings is a good healthy thing to do. It honors God and invites others into our healing.

Unusual Kindness

The Apostle Paul experienced an unusual kindness. On his journey to Rome, the ship experienced hurricane-force winds, and Paul, his fellow prisoners, and soldiers shipwrecked at Malta.

Already drained from the storm, Paul and the prisoners barely escaped death from the soldiers who feared they would all escape their imprisonment. Because the centurion wanted to spare Paul's life, he kept them from carrying out their plan.

Once the ship hit a sandbar, it began to break into pieces by the pounding of the surf. Time was of the essence, so they jumped overboard to get to shore. Stress and anxiety were at a high. They didn't know what to expect.

Cold and wet from jumping from a run-aground ship, they found kindness on the island of Malta.

The Islanders showed us unusual kindness. Acts 28:2

Not only did they find a warm welcome and kindness upon arrival, but the islanders also took care of their needs upon sailing again three months later.

People like these islanders put others ahead of themselves, taking care of needs as they see fit. People who take care of each other when circumstances threaten our sanity, our livelihood, or our physical condition become lifelong friends.

"Because he loves me," says the Lord, "I will rescue him; I will protect him, for he acknowledges my name. He will call upon me, and I will answer him. I will be with him in trouble, I will deliver him and honor him. With long life, will I satisfy him and show him my salvation." Psalm 91: 14-16

Be Thankful Because of Who God Is

God asks us to be thankful because of who He is. We can also be thankful because He gives us peace that passes all understanding.

1 Thessalonians 5:16-18 says, "Rejoice always, pray continually, give thanks in all circumstances; for this is God's will for you in Christ Jesus." Always, continually, and in all circumstances.

In the Garden of Gethsemane, Jesus didn't praise God for His circumstances. He cried out to His Father in pain, but ended with "not my will, but yours."

I don't know about you, but I often want answers to my questions right now. My guess is that you haven't gotten immediate answers to your questions from God either. However, that doesn't mean that God doesn't want you to talk to Him about it. There is no perfect formula. God will reveal His answer in His time.

It's less about answers and more about having a relationship with and being real with God. It means letting God be your everything in your time of need.

Friend, there will be hard days . . . there have been hard days. Days where you want to sit and cry until you can't cry anymore. Days where you can't breathe because the pain is too great. Days when just taking one step in front of the other is all you can accomplish. It is in those days we especially need to let Him be our strength and our shield. Those who have grieved over the death of a spouse will tell you that the raw pain eases, and is replaced by sadness. The bad days and the sadness will both eventually decrease, and the good days will increase.

Jesus is our hope and our salvation. We can trust Him to give us the strength we need for each day.

Be Thankful Because God Gives Us Peace

I could hear the sound of nature as I sat quietly at a local park on a spring morning. But when the maintenance man, oblivious to my meditation, came by with a leaf blower, the noise was all I could hear. After he passed by, I could once again hear the sound of birds chirping, squirrels scampering, and fish jumping in the pond.

Everyday distractions keep us from hearing from God and receiving His arms of comfort. They keep us busy so that we don't think about our relationship with the Lord. When we're in this state, peace alludes us. Trying to get to everything in our day may bring us to the point of checking things off our list, but if God isn't a part of our day, *then we are working in vain*. Shouldn't fellowship with God and doing things that are pleasing in His sight be one of the main goals in the Christian life?

That day in the park, I just wanted to hear silence. My plan was to get away from all the noise so I could hear God's whisper, to feel Him with me in my sadness. It was the anniversary of the day I lost my husband

and I desperately wanted God's presence with me to soothe my soul and lessen the pain in my heart.

God was with me through those few minutes as I sat there alone. He did show up. That maintenance man didn't even know he was being used by God as he walked my way. God used that experience to speak to me about the distractions in my life and how they keep me from a quality relationship with Him.

As I reflected on this, God gave me peace that morning. I left feeling protected and loved. He showed me that if I made time for Him, He would give me the wisdom to make the other hours of the day more profitable.

If any of you lacks wisdom, you should ask God, who gives generously to all without finding fault, and it will be given to you.
James 1:5

Be Thankful for the Good Days

"Go and make it a great day," Amanda, my friend and financial adviser, said as we ended a call one spring morning.

Before that, I could only describe the day as me being in a "funk." I didn't feel well and was down, tired, and frustrated.

But those six small words soaked into my being. I have the ability to make the day great by the attitude I choose to have.

Not only that, but an attitude of gratitude can even improve my health, as well as my emotional and social well-being. On the flip side, negative thoughts also impact our health and send our bodies into stress mode. Often a result of depression or insecurity, bouts of negativity can cause serious health problems and damage relationships. Some researchers believe it can lead to a weakened immune system and high blood pressure. [1]

However, studies show that the practice of adopting an attitude of gratitude brings positive effects. It can reduce the risk of heart disease, improve sleep quality, and improve relationships, as well as increase the recovery time of certain conditions and diagnoses. Overall, it makes us happier. [2]

Let's not let a rotten attitude rob us of a good day. As my friend encouraged me, we have the ability to change the outcome of our day. Let's choose gratitude.

Pray With Me

Thank you for being with me during this trial. I know I can only make it with Your help. Help me to be the mom, the daughter, the daughter-in-law, and the friend You want me to be. I recognize that there are also attacks from Satan. I must remember that You are my strength and my shield of protection from his attacks. You are my hope and my salvation. You are my reason for being here on earth. You are the ONE true God and I will trust You and praise You every day. Lord Jesus, I want to please You in all that I do. Thank you for who you are and for the peace you provide. In Jesus' name, amen.

For as members of one body you are called to live in peace, and always be thankful. Colossians 3:15 (NLT)

Be anxious for nothing, but in everything by prayer and supplication with thanksgiving let your requests be made known to God. Philippians 4:6 (ESV)

Shout for joy to the Lord, all the earth. Worship the Lord with gladness; Come before him with joyful songs. Know that the Lord is God. It is he who made us, and we are his; We are his people, the sheep of his pasture. Enter his gates with thanksgiving. And his courts with praise; give thanks to him and praise his name. For the Lord is good and his love endures forever; his faithfulness continues through all generations. Psalm 100

Questions for Reflection / Thoughts to Ponder

1. Thank God for three things in your life before getting out of bed.

2. What are some of the things you have learned to be thankful for from your experience of losing your spouse (or another type of significant loss?)

3. Remember, Jesus does not call us to be grateful for our loss but to be grateful for Him and the strength He will give us to get through it. Take a moment to think about how He has given you strength and praise Him for it.

1. https://www.chicagonow.com/spiritual-physical-wellness/2020/11/bitterness-can-hurt-your-health/

2. https://positivepsychology.com/benefits-gratitude-research-questions/

9

Hope Heals

*May the God of hope fill you with
all joy and peace as you trust in
him, so that you may overflow
with hope by the power of the Holy
Spirit. Romans 15:13*

Hope means "to look forward to with confidence and fulfillment."
It's a feeling of expectation and desire for a certain thing to happen. For someone grieving, that hope can play out in different ways.

One moment we can smile at a memory, then in an instant, tears are burning in our eyes and rolling down our cheeks. That is the way of grief. Laughter and tears, joy and sorrow.

In times of intense suffering, it's hope that gets us through the day. Let the beauty of God's work fill your heart with hope.

Hope Conquers

We can be sad about our circumstances, our loss, or even just our place in life at the moment. However, I encourage you to not lose hope. Thinking of my family's loss can still fill me with sadness, especially around holidays throughout the year. But I am also thankful that God is in my sadness.

He brings blessing and hope during our pain. He delivers us from our sorrows and because of that, we can have hope that things will get better. And having hope helps us cope.

Paul tells us that we are not "to grieve like the rest of men, who have no hope. We believe that Jesus died and rose again and so we believe that God will bring with Jesus those who have fallen asleep in him." (1 Thessalonians 4:13-14)

TRUE CALLING

I thought my youngest son, Parker, was sleeping, as he lay in the bed beside me. He was usually the one who lends perspective to situations, and true to form, he began to share his dream of wanting to be an artist one day. (That was our routine on weekends after my husband passed away. The boys would take turns staying in my room — one in my bed, the other two on the floor until they swapped the next night. This went on for a while until they were too old or it was not "cool" to do so.)

Parker was nine at the time when he reminded me of my true calling. After he talked to me about his dream, he became quiet and thoughtful. Then he turned to me and asked, "Mommy, was your dream always to be a mom?" I replied, "yes, it was."

Excitedly he said, "Then you're living your dream!"

And so I am. What a way to put things in perspective.

GOD COMES THROUGH

Because even though being a mom can be tough, especially when you're alone, I remember the days when my greatest hope in life was to have children and raise a family. I remember the stressful days when we waited on the pregnancy test results, the days when we learned about another miscarriage, and the devastating day we learned our unborn child wouldn't live once born into this world.

The first Mother's Day after our baby Ashlynn died at birth, I could hardly hold it together. My heart was so empty, the pain unbearable.

But God in His mercy dropped a baby in our lap just two months later. I met him when he was three hours old and it was love at first sight. He grabbed my finger and held on like there was no tomorrow.

Two and a half years later, we met our second son when he was one day old. And two and a half years later, I had our third son when I was 43. After that, I accepted with gratitude that I would be a boy mom. And we haven't stopped going, playing ball, and challenging each other yet. Everything and I mean everything, is a competition. You boy moms know what I'm talking about. Thank you, Lord, that I get to be a mom to these boys.

I tell you this story because many times we don't know why tragic things happen. With our world turned upside down, we are often at a loss as to what to do next.

I certainly don't know all the answers, but I do know that Jesus does. God came through for us then. And He gives us hope today to face whatever obstacle is in front of us, whatever giant we're facing, whatever fear or worry that has us bound.

I encourage you to stay strong and cling to Him. He is the one who can bring blessing from pain, joy from sorrow, and hope from crushing circumstances.

The Lord bless you and keep you: The Lord make his face to shine upon you and be gracious to you: The Lord turn his face toward you and give you peace. Numbers 6:24-26

Hope Drives Out Darkness

Sadness is a part of life. And grief can pop up without a moment's notice.

As I write this, it has been seven Christmases since my husband went to be with the Lord. As I thought about that number, I realized that with this Christmas my youngest son, who is now 14, will have as many Christmases without his daddy as he did with him. That makes my soul weary all over again. What loss and heartache. What pain. This is where I must remind myself of the truth that God cares and is in my corner.

The LORD is near to those who are discouraged; he saves those who have lost all hope. Psalm 34:18

It may not be Christmas that triggers your sadness. It may be driving by a familiar hangout or completing a familiar task. It could be stumbling upon an old photo or video, or hearing a favorite song. For me, sitting outside on my porch listening to a couple of favorite songs over and over brought on sadness but also helped me to somehow keep my husband close.

Tears stung my eyes as I sat there late one afternoon. Unexpectedly, my son Garrett and three or four friends joined me. (They have always traveled in packs, moving around from one house to the next.) They didn't know I was having a moment, and what they had stepped into. But they quickly assessed it, then talked, joked, and laughed with me. God used those teenagers to lighten my burden.

It's what we do with these memories or triggers that matter. Regardless of our loss and our current circumstances, we take one step at a time and see beyond our circumstances to find hope. Romans 12:12 says Be joyful in hope, patient in affliction, faithful in prayer.

Hope Strengthens

SETBACKS AND OBSTACLES

Toward the end of that first summer without my husband, leading up to the one-year anniversary of his passing, I began to feel anxious and overwhelmed. There were decisions to be made and it was all up to me. I had never felt so depressed in my entire life. I felt I was headed for a nervous breakdown.

I began to think I needed medicine to get me through the day. though I never did take that step to do so. (Please note, it wasn't because I'm against medicines that help people with mental health issues.)

That time in my life was as close as I had been to what I thought would be my undoing. Everything felt heavy and I felt bound by anxiety.

I decided to take a month off from work to try to get my house and life in better order. I knew about an upcoming women's retreat being held at a local church that several of my friends attended.

I remember talking about it with a friend at the soccer field and asking if registration was full. It was, but she offered to add me to the waiting list. The next day, she called and told me a spot had opened — and that I had until the next morning to decide if I wanted to take it.

I sat on my porch swing that next morning, debating on if I should go. Fear held me captive. I worried about leaving the boys with relatives over those three days. I remember saying to God that I needed a real sign . . . I needed to know clearly if He wanted me to go or stay at home.

Within seconds, I got a text from another friend who said she had heard I was thinking about attending and hoped I could go. I immediately thought about my request and took that as God's yes. That moment reminded me that God cares about every detail.

Obstacles presented themselves and almost kept me from getting on the bus that would take me to the retreat location, which was 30 minutes away from home. The enemy tried to use guilt over leaving my boys for the weekend, even using an ugly collision on our trampoline, a bloody forehead, and an almost knocked-out tooth only 20 minutes before I was supposed to be at the church!

But I did get on that bus and God used that retreat as a turning point in my life. I felt treasured and held up to the Father through prayers as well as the care given to me. A clear message that spoke directly to me was that everybody has had or currently has something devastating going on in their lives.

Some say that comparison is the thief of joy. We tend to compare our lives with others who look like they have it all together or whose life seems easy and trouble-free. That retreat was enlightening for me.

Through tears and prayers and even laughter, God gave me perspective and moved me forward in my healing journey. I believe programs like GriefShare also assist in the healing journey and I encourage you to take part if it is available in your area.

Hope Believes in a Better Tomorrow

HOPE IN MY HEART

God always speaks to me through spider lilies. There was a day early in the fall of 2001 when Matthew and I drove two hours to visit our precious daughter's grave. It had only been a few weeks since she had slipped away from our lives. . . before we even had a chance to get to know her. As we drove up to the family plot in the cemetery, her grave was covered with spider lilies, which isn't unusual that time of the year. The unusual part was that there were no spider lilies anywhere in the cemetery as far as we could see, except those on her grave. Many, many spider lilies.

God touched my heart that day and gave me hope . . . hope that He did have a better future for me. Peace about where she was and confidence in a God who cares for us, even on days when grief feels like it's sucking the life out of us.

Each year, whether driving, walking, or running, seeing spider lilies along my path reminds me of the day God placed hope in my heart.

Do you have a "thing" between you and the Lord, too? Something that you know He uses to place hope in your heart? If not, why not ask Him for eyes to see what might already be a pattern of an "inside thing" with the Lord?

A Sign from Heaven

As our 20-year wedding anniversary approached, six months after my husband's death, my work at my marketing firm grew extremely busy. Even so, I had planned to take the day off. I had not really spent quality time alone to grieve and I wanted that day all to myself with my memories and my grief. I had even told a couple of friends about my plan. But my plan did not come to fruition.

A few days before the anniversary, my mom had to visit the emergency room at our local hospital due to a cough and difficulty breathing. On the day of my anniversary, the doctor placed her on a ventilator. She was 76 at the time. Mom did get better — she fully recovered and was able to go home. However, I knew she had been really sick that week.

A few weeks later, after dropping off groceries at my parent's house, my mom stopped me as I was about to leave. She mentioned, "when you have a minute, I want to tell you something."

I was in a hurry, but I mentally put everything else aside and replied, "let's talk now." She told me that while in the hospital, there was a day she knew that she could go either way. I also knew exactly when her worst days were. She said that as she lay there, she could see a light off to the side and she thought about what she should do.

She considered my dad and how hard it would be for me to take care of him since I had recently lost my husband. Dad was 84 and needed help with daily activities. She saw my sister and thought, she couldn't die on her birthday, even though she knew it wasn't really her birthday.

Then she continued "and then I saw Matthew. And he asked me, 'what about my boys?'" She told me that was when she knew she couldn't go yet.

Thoughtful, I asked, "Mom, what do you think that means?"

She replied "I don't know. I'm just telling you what I saw." I don't know exactly what was real or not, and I certainly don't understand it, but I know that God used that experience to show my mom she was needed and gave her the desire and the drive to get better.

God also used her story to encourage me, inspire hope, and simply reflect on the wonder of it all.

Pray With Me

Thank You for Your word that gives me hope and for your blessings even when I don't deserve them. Thank You that I can live a life free from fear and that I am never truly alone. Thank You that You are a God of answered prayer and that You are *my God* in whom I can trust. You are faithful and Your grace is sufficient. My soul finds rest in You Lord; my hope comes from You. Thank You for Your comfort and Your promise of hope for the future. In Jesus' name, amen.

———————— ▲ ————————

My soul clings to you; Your right hand upholds me. Psalm 63:8 (ESV)

He who dwells in the shelter of the Most High will rest in the shadow of the Almighty. I will say to the Lord, "He is my refuge and my fortress, my God, in whom I trust. Psalm 91:1-2 (ESV)

Let us hold unswervingly to the hope we profess, for He who promised is faithful. Hebrews 10:23

"For I know the plans I have for you," declares the Lord, "plans to prosper you and not to harm you, plans to give you hope and a future. Then you will call on me and come and pray to me, and I will listen to you." Jeremiah 29:11-12

———————— ▲ ————————

Questions for Reflection / Thoughts to Ponder

1. How has God placed hope in your heart for a brighter future?

2. What setbacks and obstacles have you encountered as you have walked your journey of grief?

3. How has Satan tried to discourage you and steal your hope?

10

MY HEART SINGS

But I will sing of your strength,
in the morning I will sing of your
love; for you are my fortress, my
refuge in times of trouble, you
are my strength, I sing praise to
you; You, God, are my fortress, my
God on whom I can rely. Psalm
59:16-17

I grew up in a household where music was a constant. Raised on gospel and country music, I once dreamed of being a backup singer to Ronnie Milsap, a country music artist born blind. Although I lost sight of that dream, I did get my picture made with him as a teenager when he visited the local K-Mart.

From country to gospel to contemporary worship songs, God often ministers to me through music. Music pierces my heart, speaking to the deepest parts of my soul.

Worshipping the Lord through music moves me. It connects me with God and people as we enjoy music together. It sustained me through the death of our infant daughter and then later through the death of my husband.

The power of music provides direction, especially during difficult times. Throughout the pages of this book, I have mentioned songs that have spoken to me during my grief, and through difficult times. I encourage you to search them and listen, allowing their lyrics to minister to your soul. (See back pages for a complete song list.)

God Shows Up When Praise is Offered

King David began the first ministry of music. We see in the book of 2 Chronicles that God actually commanded him to do it. Years later, King Hezekiah purified the temple and once again incorporated music into their worship.

"He stationed the Levites in the temple of the Lord with cymbals, harps and lyres in the way prescribed by David and Gad the king's seer and Nathan the prophet; this was commanded by the Lord through his prophets." 2 Chronicles 19:25

Often, we are told to praise and worship God throughout Scripture. God Almighty, the God of the universe, the Alpha and Omega, says music plays an important role in our worship. Scripture tells us God acts in response to praise through music. King David's life epitomizes this. David praised God often. The result? 2 Chronicles 18:13 tells us that the Lord gave David victory everywhere he went.

The presence and power of God often present themselves through music. This happened with the prophet Elisha. Music ministered to Elisha before prophesying. It was common at that time to call upon musicians to calm the mind and ease stress. He would need to think clearly to discern the voice and will of God.

Elisha requested a harpist and when the harpist played, God's power was released on Elisha.

But now bring me a harpist. While the harpist was playing, the hand of the Lord came on Elisha." 2 Kings 3:15

Wow. Did you see that? I know exactly how this feels. Sometimes, while listening to a song, I can sense God's presence and He impresses upon me very clearly what He wants me to hear. I may not hear audible words, but I know beyond a shadow of a doubt that it is Him speaking. Worship takes us from focusing on ourselves to focusing on God.

Praise Delivers Us in Battle

Praise is a force to be reckoned with. Jehoshaphat was the fourth king of the Kingdom of Judah. He campaigned against idolatry and led the people to renew their worship of the One True God. He championed peace between Israel and Judah. In his desperation for God to be with his army, he appointed singers to go out before them. Their only job was to praise God through song and the playing of holy instruments.

After consulting the people, Jehoshaphat appointed men to sing to the Lord and praise him for the splendor of his holiness as they went out at the head of the army, saying:

"Give thanks to the Lord, For his love endures forever." 2 Chronicles 20: 21-22

As they began to sing and praise, the Lord set ambushes against the men of Ammon and Moab and Mount Seer who were invading Judah, and they were defeated. Don't miss this — they hadn't even won the battle yet, but they knew they would because God had told them He would deliver them.

Oh, that we would worship like that, pray like that. It may seem like we are walking right into the battle of our lives. How can we react like Jehoshaphat? As I write this, I am praying for a dear friend who will undergo double mastectomy surgery in only a few hours. I want to pray in desperation — not that God will show up because I know He is already with her, but to pray thirsting and longing for more of His presence in her life and in mine.

As the Israelites did before battle, I want to rejoice in what God will do before I even see the results.

God Moves Through Song

Another story in the New Testament illustrates the power of praising God even in the midst of a great trial. Paul and Silas were beaten and thrown into prison in Rome for casting out a spirit from a slave girl who earned a great deal of money for her owners by fortune-telling. While in prison, Paul and Silas were praying and singing hymns. They were in a desperate situation — unjustly locked up for preaching the gospel — but they still praised the Lord. They were beaten to the point they thought they would wake up in Heaven.

Here's the point. They chose to praise the Lord. They may have been in chains, but they were free to praise His name. As a matter of fact, they praised the Lord until the walls began to shake. Let's take a look at the account from the book of Acts.

About midnight Paul and Silas were praying and singing hymns to God, and the other prisoners were listening to them. Suddenly there was such a violent earthquake that the foundations of the

prison were shaken. At once all the prison doors flew open, and
everyone's chains came loose. Acts 16:25-26

I'd say that moment of audible worship completely changed the atmosphere in the walls of that prison. The men there could not have missed the power and glory of God in that moment.

And we don't want to miss the glory of God either. But for many, this season of grief is symbolic of Paul and Silas' time in prison. A place of confinement, a prison can represent different aspects of our lives like grief, sadness, bitterness, fear, worry, and anxiety. We can be bound by our own feelings and negative emotions. They can become a stronghold in our lives, trapping us in our circumstances.

But that is not where God wants us. The good news is that we don't have to stay bound by negative emotions or our circumstances. Our worship can move us from being bound to raising our minds and hearts above the stress of our circumstances and focusing on God.

The Lord is able to deliver us from every battle and trial. Worship Him in song and experience the power that can break our chains and make a way for God to move in our hearts.

Music Changes Your Life

Music can change your life forever. Countless times in my life, God has unequivocally carried me through difficulties with music. When Matthew and I found out in 2001 that our unborn baby would not live once I gave birth, God used the song by Greg Long – *In the Waiting* – to help me make it through those four heart-wrenching months.

And also as a widow, there have been many special songs that have ministered to me during my grief journey. Lauren Daigle's *Trust in You*, is another one that encourages us to let go of our worries, our trials — even our dreams — and let God have His way in our lives. When we lay them at the feet of Jesus, we have the capacity to receive His best for our lives.

This song spoke to me because its message resonated with where I was at that point in time. I was tired and weary. God didn't provide the miracle. I didn't get the answers I wanted, so I cried out to God. The truth is He knows me better than I know myself. I had to make a decision whether I was going to put complete trust in Him.

When the World Drives You to Your Knees

As I sat in the parking lot of an orthodontist's office in the fall of 2015, I first heard the song by Danny Goeke *Tell your Heart to Beat Again*. I needed to hear those words right at that time. It felt like my heart was barely beating at all. If you're in this place today, I encourage you to listen to Goeke's song as well as some of the others I've listed here. When grief has a grip on you and you're driven to your knees, remember God's grace. Praise Him. Praise escorts us right into the presence of God and opens the door to joy. It focuses us on who truly matters and frees us up to receive blessings.

The next year, Dani and Lizzy's *Dancing in the Sky* ministered to me in a different way. Then a friend sent me the song *One More Day* by Diamond Rio, which also holds special meaning to me.

Certain songs remind us of our loved ones and can stimulate our good memories in a powerful way. For me, it's *Banana Pancakes* by Jack Johnson or *Keep Going* by the Revivalists or the old hymn *Because He Lives*. Those songs had meaning to my husband. They still move me today. They bring with them fond memories — memories that usher in joy and gratefulness for the time we had together and bring about other good feelings — feelings we may not have recognized in a long time.

Sometimes music expresses the very thing that's on our hearts and can minister to us in ways a sermon cannot. Another great song, *Holy Water* by We The Kingdom, reminds me that God's forgiveness was freely given and that He is always with us. The song talks about our desperate need for God, the sweetness of His forgiveness, and the grace that makes us want to make changes in our lives.

Music Stimulates the Brain

God gave us the gift of song. Did you know that few things stimulate the brain the way music does? That's right. According to John Hopkins Medicine,[1] listening to or playing music helps keep your brain engaged throughout the aging process. It can even reduce anxiety, blood pressure, and pain, as well as improve sleep quality, mood, mental alertness, and memory.

How much more beneficial can music be when it's focused on worshipping God?

Ephesians encourages us to sing and make music from our hearts to the Lord.

Do not get drunk on wine, which leads to debauchery. Instead, be filled with the Spirit, speaking to one another with psalms, hymns, and songs from the Spirit. Sing and make music from your heart to the Lord, always giving thanks to God the Father for everything, in the name of our Lord Jesus Christ. Ephesians 5:18-20

Take the time to research and listen to your own style of praise music. You can even use these mentioned as a starting point if you'd like. There are also many other songs and hymns that inspire and encourage. Just having praise music playing somewhere in your house will uplift you and bless you.

From King David to Paul and Silas to your own version of worship in the car, music with Biblical messages and scripture soothes our minds and soul. The Word of God is our most powerful weapon against the enemy, but we have to know it for it to help break down our prison walls. Many praise and worship songs quote Scripture directly. Listening to Christian music can also be a big help in learning scripture.

Music was first ordered by God himself. It is powerful. It is healing. It produces results.

Pray With Me

Lord, I want to worship like the army of Jehoshaphat, and to pray like that. The battle already belongs to You. I want to rejoice in what You will do before I see the results. I long for You. I am desperate for You. You are Holy and worthy of our praise. Thank You for the music You've placed in our world and in our hearts. In Jesus' name, amen.

Sing a new song to the Lord! Sing His praises from the ends of the earth! Isaiah 42:10 (NLT)

Shout for joy, you heavens; rejoice, you earth; burst into song, you mountains! For the LORD comforts his people and will have compassion on his afflicted ones. Isaiah 49:13

Questions for Reflection / Thoughts to Ponder

1. How has music ministered to you during your grief? List specific songs that God has placed in your heart to give you strength and courage, hope and encouragement.

2. Praising the Lord through difficulty is a choice. Remember Paul and Silas. As they praised the Lord, they were still in prison. But their environment had certainly changed. How have you seen God work in you or your circumstances as a result of that choice to praise Him through music?

3. A musician, David was also described as Israel's beloved singer of songs. 2 Samuel 23:1 (NET) I love that! Take time now to listen to some of your favorite praise songs and allow God's presence to wash over you. If you don't have a favorite, look up and listen to some of the ones listed at the back of the book.

---

1. https://www.hopkinsmedicine.org/health/wellness-and-prevention/keep-your-brain-young-with-music

11

FRIENDS RISE TO THE OCCASION

"This is my commandment, that
you love one another as I have
loved you. John 15:12

L ife is full of ironies.

Matthew and I spent much of our time proving to our oldest son when he was a baby that the world revolved around him. Not in words, so much, but in how we treated him.

Later, with two younger brothers, we spent much of our time convincing him that the world did not revolve around him. That there are, in fact, other people to consider.

That's what friends do . . . consider others.

Friends Put Others First

I heard a story about a college professor who conducted an experiment that illustrated an important principle about finding happiness. In class one day, he gave a balloon to every student, giving the assignment to write their names on the balloon, then drop it out in the hallway. He then instructed them to find their balloon within a five-minute timeframe. Not one could do it.

Then he told the students to grab the first balloon they saw and give it to that person. This time, everyone had their own balloon within 5 minutes. The lesson in that story? When you seek to find your own happiness, it cannot be found. When you put others first, your own happiness follows.

The epistles are letters turned into books of the Bible from Romans to Jude. They were written to churches and individuals and contain the main instructions for us concerning how to walk out our Christian life. We need to receive them as a guide for our actions today. They are full of instructions related to loving one another, encouraging one another, and how to follow Jesus in everyday ways. Let's take a look at one of them.

"Be devoted to one another in love. Honor one another above yourselves." Romans 12:10

That's how God revealed himself to me in my time of need. Countless friends and members of our church community prayed for me and held me up when I didn't think I could take another breath, much less another step. I had three boys who needed me, however. They were hurting in a different way. Other family members were also hurting. After all, Matthew still had a mother, a father, a brother, a sister, and nieces and their families. I had to remember that God loved me enough to give me 20 years with my husband, loved me enough to give him a home much better than the one he had here, and loved me enough to give me assurance that I would see him again one day.

Friends Love Through Action

There were two friends who stayed with my sons while I made that last visit to the hospital. I had said goodbye the night before but went that morning to get the final confirmation from the doctor. When I came home, notes with scriptures were posted throughout my house.

Verses of encouragement and comfort were on my bathroom mirror, the laundry room wall, by my bedside table, and on doors and windows. I never took them down. Some eventually fell off and were lost over the years, but that simple act will never be forgotten. Their kindness wrapped my boys and me up in God's love.

Another friend, Beth, sent me an iPod loaded with uplifting songs. It only required me to turn it on.

With a heart as big as Texas, someone offered to mow our yard for a season and teach my boys how to maintain it when they were older. I didn't see him, but he dropped off a business card with a message after the memorial service. While my head was spinning with the events of the previous few days, God sent someone to lighten my load.

A neighbor still shows up at my back door every few months with a Ziplock bag in his hand. His words are few, just "I went fishing today and brought you some white perch." His demeanor is quiet, but his actions are loud. He wears generosity admirably, and we are blessed by it. I've learned to accept the gift and appreciate the giver (and to pan-fry white perch like a pro).

Then another friend helped me weed through and organize the financial end of things.

I also have a friend and neighbor who calls every year around Father's Day, checking if we're in town. "I want to drop off something," Julie tells me. The first few years were a variety of chocolates, which the boys and I devoured. Later, she left a healthier choice.

Many people are generous and thoughtful following the death of a loved one. But it's uncommon to continue blessing someone for six years. Her consideration of my boys, especially during a holiday when they feel the loss more, refreshes my spirit.

Another good friend still helps me out with computer technical questions and issues. And two other friends even took it upon themselves to redecorate the boys' room for me.

Someone else gave my boys 25 $1 bills in booklet form before we left on vacation one year.

Whether the need is big or small, I can count on my friend Sarah to be there. She even persuades us to dress up in Christmas pajamas for holiday cookie-making. Even when we thought my boys had outgrown the activity, they asked us when we were getting together.

Not to mention I was fortunate to have both my parents, Matthew's parents, and some other extended family living nearby, which certainly added to my comfort level and peace of mind. My father-in-law began driving the boys to their Boy Scout meetings each week. God surrounded me with people to care for me emotionally and spiritually, as well as help with the many practical details I needed to get done.

GOD REFRESHES US THROUGH PEOPLE

In a similar way, Paul tells us that the Christians in Corinth refreshed Titus' spirit.

By all this we are encouraged. In addition to our own encouragement, we were especially delighted to see how happy Titus was, because his spirit has been refreshed by all of you. 2 Corinthians 7:13

That is what God has done for me, and I bet He's done the same for you. He refreshes us through people. He restores our hope with kindness given. It may be through family, friends, and acquaintances, or the warmth and thoughtfulness of a good neighbor.

Friends love well. Don't miss the love and encouragement God delivers to your doorstep. Don't miss the joy of loving and blessing others today. Love trumps everything.

My command is this: Love each other as I have loved you. John 15:12

Friends Live Out Scripture

My oldest son Connor used to say the word tending before he could say pretending. He would tell us something that either didn't make sense or something we would question. He would respond with "I'm just tending, momma. I'm just tending."

How often do we go through the motions and pretend we're okay, instead of opening up and letting someone know our inner thoughts and fears?

Until you get to know someone on a deeper level, you often fail to notice the hurts and disappointments that bombard their lives. Sharing our lives with people, which is not something easy for me to do, brings about healing. Sometimes we need to stop pretending and be open about where we are — the good and the bad.

Let God surround you with His love by 1) opening up and letting others in and 2) being more than a surface friend to others when they are going through a rough patch.

Friends and family have lived out these scriptures to my family. God used them to lovingly pour blessing upon blessing on us. They showed us love in action, along with Biblical instruction in action.

One of the most important instructions Jesus gave his followers was recorded in John's gospel.

"A new commandment I give you: love one another. As I have loved you, so you must love one another. By this everyone will know that you are my disciples, if you love one another." John 13:34-35

Friends Pull Out All the Stops

It was a test of my patience...and a lesson in trust.

The birthday items were ordered and due to be delivered on the day of the birthday party scheduled to begin at 4 pm. The problem? I had failed to get the time of delivery. After checking the front door on and off all day, worry began creeping in, and eventually, I was in an all-out panic!

The online tracking information told me the package had made it to my hometown and was on the delivery truck by 8 am. So I assumed (incorrectly) that it would make it on time. How could I have let this happen? I remember naming myself the "worst mom ever" that day.

When I left for the party 30 minutes early, I called my dear friend and neighbor, Angela, and asked her to check again before she left for the party, to which she answered, "You know UPS doesn't deliver on our street until 5:30 or 6:00?" My anxiety raised about 100 levels. By then, the party would be over! Four-thirty came and went and no package had arrived. Not only did Angela wait for my package, she also drove around the neighborhood, stalking the delivery truck.

In the meantime, another friend, Sarah, who was at the party, talked with UPS on the phone, attempting to find out what we needed to do to intercept the package from the delivery truck. She had my driver's license in hand, ready to pose as me in order to meet the truck and convince the driver to hand over the package . . . as soon as Angela figured out which truck in fact had the package on board.

Sarah never had to leave because Angela not only tracked down the truck, she convinced the driver that he must give her the package because a five-year-old toe-headed little boy (waiting to turn into the gold ranger) needed power ranger decorations to complete the party.

My story may be a little overdramatic but bear with me. When Angela walked through the door, package-in-hand, God impressed upon me the value and blessing of friendship.

How often do we pull out all stops to help a friend in need? How often do we know someone so well that we anticipate what they need before they ask? Or how often do we venture beyond surface conversation and really get to know someone? I am so thankful for the friends God has placed in my life — to live life with, laugh with, pray with, celebrate with, cry with, and mourn with.

As I began to reflect on my blessings that day, God brought to my mind scriptures that calmed my fears, lifted me up, and soothed my soul. Blessings that were freely given, even when I didn't deserve them.

King Solomon, the wisest man at the time, wrote:

There are 'friends' who destroy each other, but a real friend sticks closer than a brother. Proverbs 18:24 (NLT)

Friends Live Intentionally

I am such a rule follower. Sometimes to a fault. And sometimes, that tendency causes me to lose common sense.

When purchasing school supplies one fall, I searched the 5th-grade list and bought the items mentioned there. I did notice that pencils were not on the list but thought there must be some other provision for 5th graders. I was wrong.

Disappointed, my son came home the afternoon of the first day of school and exclaimed, "Mom, you didn't pack any pencils!" How could I have missed that? I searched the list again and saw that they weren't listed there. But I should have known! The child needed pencils for school.

Oh, that I would open my eyes and see what's beyond the words on a piece of paper.

How often do we hear what's not being said, see what's not being shown? Being more intentional in our relationships starts us in the right direction.

We can easily get busy with life, checking items off our list, doing who knows what. That we would open our eyes and see what's written beyond the surface of our relationships, beyond a simple greeting . . . and especially beyond an "I'm fine" to seeing a need God wants us to meet.

JESUS LIVED ON PURPOSE

Jesus was intentional. He demonstrated this throughout His walk on earth. We have much to learn from His example.

Jesus didn't have to go through the town of Samaria when traveling to or from Judea or Galilee. As a matter of fact, all the other Jews went out of their way to avoid going through Samaria. But Jesus traveled that way on purpose. He knew what awaited Him there at the well.

She was on a routine errand. Walking to the well to replenish her water supply, the Samaritan woman expected nothing out of the ordinary. When Jesus asked her for a drink of water, she stopped to listen. And she was rewarded big for it. She went to get water, but she got so much more.

Scripture says that in her excitement over finding the Messiah, she wanted to tell someone. What she did next changed her community. She left her water jar, went back to town, and shared her discovery with her village. Scripture says many from that town believed because of the woman's testimony. (John 4:39-42)

The woman at the well was never the same again.

JESUS LIVED ON TIME

Have you noticed that Jesus was always on time, yet never seemed to be in a hurry?

When He was told that Lazarus was sick, Jesus knew that time was of the essence. But He was intentional about when He arrived at their home. He wanted God's glory to be revealed.

While walking with Jarius to his home to heal his daughter, Jesus stopped along the way to talk with the woman who was healed when she touched his cloak. It didn't make sense to the disciples and others around Him, but it was intentional.

Jesus was intentional when he sought out John the Baptist to baptize him.

He was also intentional when he walked that Roman road carrying a cross.

My friends, if we are to complete the race God has given us to run, we must get rid of sin and weights. I hope that this book will help you unload the things that weigh you down, including grief. God still has a call on your life and a purpose for your being here.

Let us be intentional in our response to Jesus. Let's be intentional in our relationships, and in reaching out. Let's be intentional in throwing all that binds us aside and truly worship Him in spirit and in truth.

Friends Live With Compassion

Everybody needs a Barnabas in their life. When other disciples kept Saul from entering their circle, Barnabas vouched for him.

Saul had led the great persecution against the church in Jerusalem, dedicating himself to destroying Christians. Newly converted, Saul, now Paul, offered to help those he had recently persecuted. Those leaders, in turn, refused to accept him as a brother in the Lord. In fact, they were still hiding from him. Except for one.

When he came to Jerusalem, he tried to join the disciples, but they were all afraid of him, not believing that he really was a disciple. But Barnabas took him and brought him to the apostles. Acts 9:26-27

Barnabas defended Paul. He bravely brought him in and introduced him to the brothers.

How did Barnabas know he could trust Paul? No doubt he had heard stories of how the believers in Damascus had been persecuted. He discerned that Paul's conversion experience was genuine and recognized God's work in his life.

Barnabas had a godly reputation, being described as a "good man, full of the Holy Spirit and faith." (Acts 11:24) He had compassion for the poor, was a man of faith, and was obedient to the promptings of the Holy Spirit. While the others focused on Paul's past, Barnabas looked beyond to Paul's future. He saw God's work in him and how he could be used to accomplish God's purpose.

Barnabas offered support and encouragement, not only then but later as they traveled together throughout the Mediterranean world to share the Gospel.

Barnabas also took a chance on another friend in the ministry. He wanted John, also called Mark, to join them as they revisited the towns where they had preached to see how the new converts and churches were doing. Mark had deserted them on a previous journey and not continued in the work. Barnabas was willing to give him a second chance, but Paul did not.

Barnabas was strong in his faith and practiced what he believed. He was a respected leader and engaged in the ministry of the church. He was an encourager and saw the good in people.

We need people like Barnabas in our lives. Not only that, we may need to be a Barnabas to someone else. God may plan to use you once you heal in ways you never imagined. Even in your grief and sorrow, I encourage you to reach out to others in need. Doing so blesses you as much as it does the recipient! During the holidays, my sons and I have volunteered at the local senior center handing out food. Even though one morning was bitterly cold, we left with our hearts overflowing with gratitude and joy.

Your love has given me great joy and encouragement, because you, brother, have refreshed the hearts of the Lord's people. Philemon 1:7

Friendship – Drop by Drop

"We cannot tell the precise moment when friendship is formed. As in filling a vessel drop by drop, there is at last a drop which makes it run over; so in a series of kindnesses there is at last one which makes the heart run over." Attributed to James Boswell in the book "The Life of Samuel Johnson."

I framed this quote and gave it to my best friend in 1995. A few months later, I married him. We left the church on a crisp, cold day in early March filled with excitement over the next journey of our lives. We drove my red BMW with two bikes mounted on the back, which was definitely a red flag to the nice, small-town policeman who gave us a speeding ticket that afternoon. We thought he might show mercy when he saw we were driving to our honeymoon destination, but unfortunately, he just wished us well as he walked off.

We were always full speed ahead. Neither of us ever dreamed of where that journey would take us. I don't regret one bit of it, for God always saw us through the good and the bad. I am thankful for every laugh, every tear, every memory, every trip together, and every friend and their impact on our lives.

God still refreshes my soul, encourages me through family and friends, and helps me through the good times and the sad times. Through friends, He helps us see something beautiful in an otherwise tragic moment.

Pray With Me

Oh my soul, thank You Jesus that I am not alone. Your presence soothes my soul. Thank You for the blessing of friendship. You are good in the happy times. You are good in the sad times. You are good. Thank You for going out of Your way — on purpose — to meet my needs. Help me to be intentional and real in my relationships with others. I pray that You will use me to be the friend that uplifts and pulls out all stops to help others in need. In Jesus' name, amen.

Questions for Reflection / Thoughts to Ponder

1. Take a moment to reflect on the friendships that have helped you through your time of grief. What stands out about those relationships? Do you have a Barnabas in your life?

2. Who do you know on a deeper level? Have you opened up and let others in?

3. Think of someone who needs your friendship right now. Reach out and let God use you to refresh and encourage someone else . . . and be blessed in return!

Part 3

Surrender and Find Peace

12

TRUST GOD'S TIMING

*There is a time for everything, and
a season for every activity under
the heavens. Ecclesiastes 3:1*

I don't know your story or what brought you to this place of grief in
your life, but here's what I do know. Everyone has something they
are going through. And while it's easier said than done, I truly believe
that surrendering to God is the key to peace in our darkest hours.

Surrender means submitting to someone else's authority. Surrendering to God means trusting His timing, all while not knowing the outcome or when an answer will even arrive. It means trusting that God's
word has never failed ... and never will. If He gave you a promise, then
He will do it in His time. While we may not understand His timing, we
can trust it. We can count on His faithfulness.

Surrender means casting our cares on Him, really giving them to
Him, and leaving them there. It means not allowing yourself to dwell
on thoughts that are contrary to God's word. It means not taking action
to try to resolve a situation that you've handed over to God. This has

become a daily decision for me. What does casting our cares look like? For me, I write in my journal those worries, fears, different situations, and plans, giving them to the Lord. Sometimes I pick them back up again. However, I believe this daily routine helps keep me grounded and serves as a reminder that I've already given that situation to the Lord.

Trust That God's Got Us

Trusting God's timing takes patience. But rest assured, God knows the past, present and future. There are more than 3,000 promises in scripture and He is faithful to all of them. We can put our trust in His hands to lead and guide us.

"For all of God's promises have been fulfilled in Christ with a resounding "Yes!" And through Christ, our "Amen" (which means "Yes") ascends to God for his glory." 2 Corinthians 1: 20 (NLT)

"The Lord is trustworthy in all he promises and faithful in all he does." Psalm 145:13

Sitting on a plane about to head to Atlanta, then on to Vermont, my 9-year-old at the time leaned over to me and whispered loudly, "I sure hope the pilot is not drunk." Me too, I thought. It's amazing that we willingly and quickly put our trust in a pilot not knowing his or her health concerns, vices, habits, etc, yet it is difficult for us to trust God for His will and His timing. We can rest assured that God, the creator of the universe, has our back.

Mark Batterson writes that the purpose of prayer is not to get what you want; but rather, to discern what God wants. In Batterson's book *Draw the Circle, the 40 Day Prayer Challenge*[1] guides the reader through this very goal. It's not about giving orders, but getting orders from God. (day 39) Batterson believes that our biggest problem is our small view of God, who is much bigger than our problems. He is much better than our best thoughts and infinitely wiser, more gracious, and more powerful than anything we can imagine.

Know therefore that the Lord your God is God, the faithful God who keeps covenant and steadfast love with those who love him and keep his commandments, to a thousand generations.
Deuteronomy 7:9 ESV

As I mentioned earlier, we got a puppy in 2022. Our puppy is little but has a big attitude. His has a demanding, "I want my way now" kind of attitude. Submission is not his strength.

That's relatable, isn't it? For most of us, submission is not a strong part of our character either. It is difficult for us to say the words "not my will, but yours." How many times have we submitted our will to God only to take back control later?

Take stress, for instance. I gave my stress about a situation to God one morning. But it wasn't long before I was worrying over and trying to control the very same situation myself!

Trust He Will Guide Us

I have a secret . . . I can't dance. No, that's not the secret. If you know me well, you know dancing is not a natural ability for me. That footwork gets me every time. I'm a dancer wannabe. I started taking dance lessons in the Spring of 2022 but didn't tell anyone for a long time. Finally, I dropped my guard and shared it with two people after seven weeks of lessons.

I've always wanted to dance well. I figure if I'm going to worship and dance before the Lord in Heaven, I'd better go ahead and learn here on earth.

One lesson took place on what would have been my 26th wedding anniversary. Memories came flooding back of the few times my husband and I danced at weddings and symphony "pops" concerts. That man could dance. Me? I would become a bumbling, stumbling, giggling mess. As I giggled, he would tell me to follow his lead. If I would do just that, we were in good shape. If I lost my focus and got out of step, well, graceful was not a word that would have been used to describe us.

My dance instructor often reminds me to wait, saying he will guide me in what to do next. I succeed for a while, but when I begin to anticipate his next move and jump ahead, I get out of step and stumble. If I've heard the word once, I've heard it a hundred times. Wait.

That's often what God asks of us too, isn't it? Wait. Follow His lead. Don't get ahead of Him. When we wait on His next move, our steps flow as they should. When we anticipate what's next, and move ahead on our own, we falter and fail.

As a new believer in Christ, it may be more difficult to discern God's voice than when we're older in the Lord.

But when we're in sync with God, life is beautiful. That is when we hang on and enjoy the experience.

My friend, moments of joy await you when you're in sync with the Father. Imagine yourself in the arms of Jesus, waltzing through life. Let His strong arms and hands guide you. Let His feet take you to places of inspiration and beauty. Let His words give you hope.

Live With a "Because You Say So" Mindset

Luke's gospel records the story of Jesus beside the Lake of Gennesaret, where fishermen were washing their nets. He got in Simon Peter's boat to speak to the people gathered there. After He taught, Jesus asked Peter to put the nets out in deep water to catch some fish. Peter knew there wasn't anything to catch out there because he and the other disciples had just fished all night without success. But he cast them anyway.

Simon answered, "Master, we've worked hard all night and haven't caught anything. But because you say so, I will let down the nets." Luke 5:5

They caught so many fish that their nets began to break and their fellow fishermen had to come to help them! After emptying their nets, not one, but two boats were so full of fish that they began to sink.

Consider also the story of the 10 lepers in Luke 17. As Jesus was going through a village on His way to Jerusalem, He met 10 lepers. They called out to Jesus from a distance and begged for pity.

When he saw them, he said, "Go, show yourselves to the priests." And as they went, they were cleansed. Luke 17:14

They obeyed Jesus before they saw the result. They were cleansed as they went to the priests. The sad part of this story is that only one came back to express gratitude. But they all believed and followed Jesus' instructions. They didn't take time to interpret, they literally just did what He said.

This is so important. When we are overcome with negative emotions, it's difficult to obey — especially when we can't see a possible outcome. These men didn't question Jesus' power. They trusted Him, obeyed His instructions, and were cleansed as they went.

"BECAUSE I SAY SO"

Moses questioned God when he was asked to lead the Israelites out of Egypt, convinced he didn't have the ability to speak to Pharoah. God had to provide another solution because Moses lacked confidence. He failed to look to God and looked at his own inadequacies instead.

Do we try to find ways to avoid obedience and make Jesus' words of no effect? The Bible very clearly gives us instructions. They're right there in black and white, and even red. (Jesus' words are in red.)

I am sorry to say that I have conveniently ignored the clear instruction of the Word of God many times. I've read that there are between 1200 and 1500 ifs in the Bible, depending on the translation. If we want God to move on our behalf, sometimes there are things we need to do.

Not only are we to obey the written Word of God, but as we mature, God expects us to walk in the Spirit which means discerning His leading and guidance, and choosing to walk accordingly.

I have often lived in a "because I say so" frame of mind, ignoring the "check in my spirit" and plowing ahead my own way. For example, I once bought a red BMW. I think I was going through a mid-life crisis early at 31! That car was so out of character for me. I had driven a Honda 2-door Accord for six years. I loved that car. I have a friend who would loosely quote scripture and say we are all in one accord when we would pile into it.

There was nothing wrong with the Accord, except I thought it was too old and had too many miles on it. As a single person, the thought of it breaking down scared me. I wanted something new and different.

Oh, I prayed about it. However, I did all the talking, with little listening. I took a friend with me to look at it and take it for a test drive. He was excited about driving it. Deep down in my heart, however, I had no peace. I bought it anyway, putting down quite a lot of money I had saved. I thought I was really something driving around in that red sports car. As a side note, so you'll know I really was in a life crisis, I also cut my hair short (first time ever) and started dating someone younger than me (which I said I would never do).

Why did God care that I bought that car? Did He even care? I believe it was an act of disobedience on my part. I just couldn't wait. And oh, I should have. It was a borderline lemon from the start. They may have been small issues, but they were a pain in the neck and in the pocketbook. The engine was good, which kept it off official "lemon" status.

A year later, I traded it, after my "younger" boyfriend, then husband Matthew, got tired of me complaining. I lost most of that down payment — a hard lesson to learn.

My point? I don't know why God told me no. But had I listened to Him, I'm sure He would have had a better solution for me. What blessing did I miss because I was disobedient? Think about the peace I gave up. I knew from the moment I drove that red car off the lot to the day I said goodbye to it that I hadn't acted in God's will. It left that much of an impression on me that I still remember the event and am writing about it more than 25 years later!

Keep Your Heart Tuned in to the Lord

Let's talk about two other Bible characters who were determined to do things their way.

King Saul lost his way sometime during his reign. What a sad, pitiful end to his life, a result of Saul's disobedience recorded in 1 Samuel 31. When did his disobedience start? For truly he was chosen by God to be Israel's first king. (1 Samuel 9-10). His downhill journey started when David got more credit and praise than Saul. Saul then became jealous of David, setting in motion his quest to kill David.

Solomon, David's son and the author of the book of Proverbs, was the wisest man that lived. Until he wasn't. Even Solomon in his old age turned his heart after other gods. He was greater in riches and wisdom than any other king of the earth yet allowed other gods in his life through his foreign wives (and he had many of them!). This ultimately caused his downfall.

So Solomon did evil in the eyes of the Lord; he did not follow the Lord completely, as David his father had done. 1 Kings 11:6

Lord, help us to remember that those small steps of disobedience matter. One step leads to the next, and that one leads to the next until you do not recognize yourself. In some cases, that first drink can lead to a lifetime of alcoholism, a second glance could lead to adultery, which could lead to a divorce and children growing up in a broken home. A decision to go against God's will could lead to a lifetime of rebellion. Obedience leads to peace and joy, while sin always leads to hurt and heartache.

According to Acts 13:52, the disciples were filled with joy and the Holy Spirit right after they were expelled from the region of Pisidian Antioch. So why were they filled with joy? I have to believe it was because they had been obedient to the Lord by speaking the truth and encouraging the church there.

Talk Less. Listen More.

Sometimes we need to stop talking . . . and listen.

Jesus once took Peter, James, and John to a mountain to pray. As He prayed, Jesus' appearance changed — His face shone like the sun and His clothing became white as light. Moses and Elijah appeared with Him. At that point, Peter suggested building three shelters — one for Jesus, one for Moses, and one for Elijah.

The title of an old country song — *When You Say Nothing At All* — says it best I think (pun intended). Maybe that's what Peter should have done - stopped talking and listened first. Because God Himself spoke from a cloud "This is my son, whom I love; with him I am well pleased. Listen to him!"

God was right there with the disciples and in His authority made a statement. No one could compare to His son.

When you're in the presence of Almighty God, I encourage you to be silent, still and listen.

A big part of finding healing for your grief and a renewed purpose for your life involves listening to God. I believe sometimes He will only speak when we are really focused on listening to Him.

Over the years, I have tried to be a better listener to God's voice. I have certainly failed again and again, but have always been blessed when I have listened and obeyed.

I want to be in a "because you say so" frame of mind toward God and have a yielded posture. Circumstances don't always make sense, but when I hear the voice of Jesus, and sense His direction, I'd best do it. I want to do it. When we hear the voice of God, we need not listen to any other voice.

Writing this book was that step for me. For years, I put it off, thinking God was not calling me. I am a private person, so the thought of sharing my inner thoughts, struggles, and pain with anyone struck fear in my heart.

When I finally did take that step of faith to leave my career and follow this calling, unexpected expenses and circumstances had me questioning the wisdom of that decision. But I held fast to my belief that I had acted on the path God had laid out for me.

When God blesses us with His presence, let's talk less and listen more.

Recognize God's Faithfulness

Looking back, the years since Matthew passed away have been a blip in time and yet also feel like an eternity. My boys and I have seen sorrow and pain, but also comfort. We've experienced milestones and setbacks. We've had times when we were at our worst, but also times of deep joy. Tears, but also laughter. Failures, yet accomplishments too. Fear and anxiety as well as confidence. I still feel an emptiness without Matthew in my life, but also a sense of gratefulness for the years we had together. I can rest knowing that one day we will see each other again.

Through it all, God has been faithful and has proven Himself trustworthy. Struggles will come, but with Jesus, we never walk alone. He will never leave us on our own.

My husband's death drew a line in the sand when it came to matters of time. Every event is now determined by whether the event happened before my husband's death in 2015 or after. I can remember any date by remembering how close it was to either before or after his passing. Strange, but it is true. Everything is either pre or post-that day when our world changed forever. But the thing that stands out is that my sons and I haven't walked alone. While we may not understand God's timing, we can trust in His faithfulness.

God is a promise keeper! He is faithful. He will supply all our needs as we surrender our will to his. We can trust His timing.

Pray With Me

Lord, I pray that you would give me the desire to do whatever You say, just because You say it. Not because it makes sense to me, but because I want to listen to Your voice and Yours alone. You are trustworthy and faithful. Help me to remain strong, and firm, and believe that You will work everything out for Your glory. Help me to do what I say, to dream bigger, love deeper, to pray bolder, listen, and plan the activities of my life in Your will. In Jesus' name, amen.

---

a time to weep and a time to laugh, a time to mourn and a time to dance Ecclesiastes 3:4

You turned my wailing into dancing; you removed my sackcloth and clothed me with joy, that my heart may sing your praises and not be silent. LORD my God, I will praise you forever. Psalm 30:11-12

I wait for the LORD, my soul waits, and in His word I put my hope. Psalm 130:5

I will instruct you and teach you in the way you should go; I will counsel you and watch over you. Psalm 32:8

Questions for Reflection / Thoughts to Ponder

1. What about trusting God challenges you the most?

2. Do you have a "because you say so" moment? Describe it. Do your wants and desires line up with God's? In what areas of your life do you need to submit to His will?

3. Give an example of God's faithfulness to you in your grief journey.

---

1. Batterson, M. (2012, December 9). Draw the Circle: The 40 Day Prayer Challenge (11.9.2012). Zondervan.

13

Miracles Happen

Jesus replied, "What is impossible
with man is possible with God."
Luke 18:27

If I tell my children to do something, that doesn't always mean it gets
done. Sometimes it may take several reminders. And sometimes I
may finally give up and do it myself.

Miracles Happen When God Speaks

I the Lord have spoken, and I will do it. Ezekiel 17:24

But beginning with the — well, the beginning — God spoke things
into existence. "Let there be light" and there was light. "Let there be an
expanse between the waters to separate water from water." And it was
so.

If the Lord says it, then it is done. There are countless examples in the Bible where Jesus' words were the turning point. He spoke it and it was done. And people were never the same.

Let's look at a few examples.

JONAH

God called Jonah to preach to the city of Ninevah. But Jonah ran away and boarded a ship for Tarshish. He didn't get far because the Lord sent a great wind and he eventually ended up in the belly of a great fish. Then the Lord commanded the fish to vomit him out.

And the lord commanded the fish, and it vomited Jonah onto dry land. Jonah 2:10

After that experience, Jonah then obeyed the Lord. I think we would be ready to obey too after living in the belly of a fish for three days and three nights.

LAZARUS

Jesus' friend Lazarus had been in the tomb for four days when Jesus raised him from the dead. Jesus was deeply moved and wept. His plan was to show them the glory of God. And that's what He did.

"Lazarus, come out!" John 11:43

Lazarus, Mary, and Martha were never the same.

CANA CRISIS

Jesus' first miracle occurred at a wedding in the village of Cana in Galilee. They were running out of wine when Jesus stepped in and saved the day. (John 2:11)

"Fill the jars with water." John 2:7

After Jesus turned the water into wine, the disciples were never the same. There Jesus showed His glory, and His disciples put their faith in Him.

MUD MIRACLE

Jesus encountered a blind man as He traveled and taught. The man was born blind. Jesus' disciples asked who had sinned — the man's parents or him. There was a purpose, Jesus said, that the work of God might be displayed in his life. Jesus spoke to the man.

"Go," he told him, "wash in the Pool of Siloam." John 9:7

Later, verse 38 tells us "then the man said, Lord I believe," and he worshipped Him. The man born blind was never the same.

After God lays His hand on us, we are never the same.

BASKET BLESSINGS

Because they had seen Jesus perform miraculous signs on the sick, a great crowd followed Jesus and His disciples to a mountainside. Jesus tested His disciples, asking them where to buy bread for the people to eat. Of course, they did not have the resources to buy enough food for all the people gathered there.

Andrew spoke up, claiming a boy had five small loaves and two small fish. I love this. Every time that Andrew is mentioned in scripture, he's bringing someone to Jesus.

Jesus took that small offering and fed everyone—and there were even leftovers.

When they had all had enough to eat, he said to his disciples, "Gather the pieces that are left over. Let nothing be wasted." John 6:12

There were 12 baskets of bread left over!

I'm not usually one to enjoy leftovers. But when I read the miracle of the 5,000, the significance of those 12 baskets of leftovers doesn't escape me. Jesus spoke it. And it was done. The people then began to say, "Surely this is the Prophet who is to come into the world." (verse 14)

With all the good He did, Jesus encountered resistance along the way, especially from religious people. After He traveled home, people took offense at Him because He had taught in the synagogue with great wisdom. According to Matthew's gospel, Jesus said "only in his hometown and in his own house is a prophet without honor." And he did not do many miracles there because of their lack of faith. (Matthew 13:57-58)

Throughout the gospels, there is a correlation between a person's faith and receiving miracles. I don't want my lack of faith to keep me from experiencing His miracles in my life.

On His last day on earth after hanging on a cross for about six hours, Jesus said "It is finished." And it was done. Scripture says, "with that, he bowed his head and gave up his spirit." (John 19:30) He had done what He came to do so that we could receive salvation and become a joint heir with Him.

Throughout Scripture when Jesus says it, it gets done. He speaks not only with love but with authority and boldness. Oh, that we would pray

with boldness and expect good things, remembering to thank God —
and tell others about it — when our prayers are answered.

Miracles Happen When Prayer is Present

I AM WILLING!

One morning, my 14-year-old son stayed home from school because he
wasn't feeling well. He ran a fever the night before. After I returned home
from an errand, he told me he felt worse, so I began to get very concerned.
It was during an outbreak of Covid in our community. That morning I
read from Luke chapter five about Jesus healing a leper.

Let's take a look at that story.

While Jesus was in one of the towns, a man came along who was
covered with leprosy. When he saw Jesus, he fell with his face to the
ground and begged him, "Lord, if you are willing, you can make me
clean." Jesus reached out his hand and touched the man. "I am willing,"
he said. "Be clean!" And immediately the leprosy left him. Luke 5:12-13

In that moment, I prayed that same prayer, "Lord, if you are willing,
make Parker well today." I finished my quiet time, then headed up the
stairs to check on him.

He was on his way down and said to me. "Mom, I don't know what
just happened, but all of a sudden I feel fine! It was about 15 minutes
ago." I told him that I knew what had happened. I shared with him my
prayer to which he replied, "that's cool."

Immediately, I began to try to rationalize — or maybe it was Satan
placing doubt in my mind. The medicine must be working . . . Or it
must have been a 24-hour thing. . . Maybe it was a fluke and he'll feel bad
again later. But then I corrected myself — I was not going to go there. I
was going to receive his immediate recovery as a direct gift from God, an
answer to prayer. I prayed boldly and God answered!

Many times I think we assume that the good things that happen around us or to us are coincidences or luck. But I believe that God still answers prayer, and we need to recognize those answers for what they are.

Count on It

You may wonder why I am discussing miracles in a book about finding joy after loss. You are likely reading this book because God didn't heal or protect your loved one from death.

Your miracle may not be baskets of leftover fish and bread, but remember, God can reveal miracles in different forms.

Your miracle might be a financial gift dropped off at the right time. It could be a changed heart. Or a phone call when you need it most. It could be a cherished memory that washes over you at just the right moment to give you extra strength for the day. A lost ring miraculously shows up. It could be a simple answer to prayer.

It could be the moment when God's great love reaches down and surrounds us, and comforts us. It could be a long-needed moment of laughter in our home.

If Jesus said it then we can count on it. We can be confident in the power we have through Him. We can rest in the knowledge that when He says He's with us, He's with us. When He says He is our strength in times of trouble, He is our strength in times of trouble. When He says we can still experience a full life, then we can.

We can expect a miracle even when we don't know how God will provide it. We don't want a lack of faith to keep us from experiencing the miracle He wants to give.

Knowing God and knowing He can be trusted also helps us to be bold when we're presented with an opportunity to share our faith or to witness through our actions. We can live in victory and not only have an abundant life here on earth but have a place prepared for us so that one day we will be with Him.

Miracles Happen When We Pray Expectantly

The twelfth chapter of Acts tells us of Peter's miraculous escape from prison. While he was there, many people gathered to pray at the house where Mary, the mother of John, lived. After the angel delivered Peter from prison, he showed up at this gathering. Scripture says they were astonished. Why were they surprised when Peter showed up?

I think the most amazing part of this passage occurs when Peter and the angel were leaving the prison. As they approached the iron gates leading to the city, the gates opened by themselves. It sounds like a Scooby Doo mystery movie, right? Imagine Peter's surprise. Of course, at that time, Peter was still thinking he was seeing a vision!

When we pray, we need to pray expecting God to answer.

One week, I decided that God had spoken to me about praying expectantly. Concerning having a family, I would often think of the negative outcomes that could happen because of my pregnancy history. My best friend had recently told me she wanted me to pray believing that she could be healed of cancer. She didn't want a doubt in my mind.

So that was the prompting for me to commit to praying like that. A week later, God challenged me on that pledge.

I found out I was pregnant at 42. Matthew and I had wanted another child. We had adopted two boys and had even talked about adopting again. After four miscarriages and a baby that died at birth, we did not have a good track record.

That day though, I decided that I would not assume I couldn't carry our baby. In past pregnancies, with our history and my age, and probably to shield myself from another disappointment, I had prayed hoping that

God would give us a healthy baby. This time, I prayed expecting good things to come. I thanked the Lord and praised him.

God answered my prayer with an 8-pound 10-ounce baby boy who only gave me a short warning that he was ready to be delivered! In 1 hour and 47 minutes (with only 30 minutes of that time actually in the hospital), that baby made his entrance into the world. And our lives were never the same.

That experience deepened my faith.

Miracles Happen When Faith is Firm

While in Iconium, Paul and Barnabas' spoke so effectively that a great number of Jews and Gentiles believed. The Jews who refused to believe stirred up the Gentiles and poisoned their minds against them. Upon learning of a plot to stone them, Paul and Barnabas fled to the cities of Lystra and Derbe to continue to preach.

There they encountered a man crippled in his feet, who listened to Paul as he was speaking. Paul looked directly at him, saw that he had faith to be healed, and called out "Stand up on your feet!" At that, the man jumped up and began to walk.

The crowd in Lystra shouted, "the gods have come to us in human form," calling Barnabas, Zeus, and Paul, Hermes. (Zeus was known as the Greek god of thunder, lightning, rain, and winds, while Hermes was considered an Olympian deity and herald of the gods.) You can read the account in Acts 14.

Of course, Paul and Barnabas were horrified, tearing their clothes and explaining they were only men who were bringing the Good News. But even then, they had difficulty keeping the crowd from offering sacrifices to them, going so far as to bring bulls and wreaths from the temple of Zeus which was located outside the city.

The very next sentence starts with "then." Then some Jews came from the cities of Antioch and Iconium (the ones who refused to believe) and won the crowd over. They stoned Paul and dragged him outside the city, thinking he was dead. (Verse 19)

The crippled man demonstrated a firm faith. Paul could even see his faith in his face. The Lycaonians did not have a real faith, jumping from one emotional event (offering sacrifices to the men) to another (stoning them). They got caught up in the moment of the miraculous and then got swayed by some misplaced passionate and persuasive Jews who wanted to harm Paul and Barnabas.

The cripple man not only left walking, but he surely left stronger in his faith. How could he not?

The question for us is the same — How deep is our faith? Do we connect with the Lord at a deeper level? Or are we going through the motions? I have certainly been at different points on this faith spectrum during my life. Difficulties have been the springboard to get me to a deeper place many times. Trials are the catalyst that causes us to go beyond our familiar and safe faith to a deep-rooted faith.

MIRACLE IN ACTION

Was that the end of the story with Paul?

No, it wasn't. Paul wasn't dead.

After the disciples had gathered around him, he got up and went back into the city. The next day he and Barnabas left for Derbe. (verse 20)

I'd like to think that Paul's getting up from that stoning was another miracle in action. Through the power of the Holy Spirit, Paul healed the man from Lystra, and the power of the Holy Spirit picked him up from being a human heap outside the city to walk his way back in.

No, Paul was "not dead." After preaching in other cities, Paul and Barnabas returned to Lystra to strengthen and encourage the disciples there to remain true to the faith. He encouraged the believers in Lystra to deepen their faith, as well as believers throughout the Gentile world.

Let us, too, allow our loss to strengthen and deepen our faith. Then, we can go on to strengthen others who have put their trust in Christ. Even Paul encourages Christians who've been comforted to comfort others.

Praise be to the God and Father of our Lord Jesus Christ, the Father of compassion and the God of all comfort, who comforts us in all our troubles, so that we can comfort those in any trouble with the comfort we ourselves receive from God. 2 Corinthians 1:3-4

Let's make faithfulness and usefulness our priority. Joy will come. I encourage you to find joy through encouraging and comforting others.

Think about it. Even though God healed Paul, he must have physically suffered a lot - almost being stoned to death! But did that deter him from serving God? Neither should our great loss deter us from serving God.

Miracles Happen Every Day

My boys loved the story about Naaman found in 2 Kings 5. A commander in the army of the king of Aram, Naaman was well-respected as a valiant soldier. However, he had leprosy. Scripture tells us of Naaman visiting the prophet Elisha and how his flesh became clean again like that of a young boy.

No doubt about it, Naaman experienced a miracle. But consider this. There were several miracles that led up to his body being restored that day. Let's take a look at them.

There was a young girl from Israel who had been taken captive. She was a prisoner in Naaman's home, serving his wife. Yet she was the one who suggested to his wife that a prophet in Samaria could cure Naaman. Even in her circumstances, she allowed herself to be used by God. She wanted the best for Naaman, to see him healed.

This was a miracle of the heart.

I believe the second miracle in this story was the simple fact that Naaman listened to her. He even petitioned the king, requesting permission to travel to see Elisha. With his importance in the land, listening to a young girl could not have been common in that day.

Naaman made the trip, but he expected praise and fanfare. You can imagine his disappointment when he was told — not by Elisha — but by Elisha's servant, to go wash seven times in the Jordan River. He left that conversation angry, questioning how washing in the Jordan could be any better than washing in any other waters in Israel.

This brings us to what I believe is the third miracle — the fact that he listened to people who were at a much lower level in society than him. They talked him off the ledge so to speak, encouraging him to do what Elisha said to do.

Once Naaman obeyed the prophet's instruction, God healed Naaman physically. Not only that, but he also healed him spiritually. Naaman said your servant will never again make burnt offerings and sacrifices to any other god but the Lord (2 Kings 5:17). All because of the heart of a young captive girl.

Let's try not to miss our everyday miracles. We want to see God in the big things — healing from sickness or disease, recovery from financial devastation, or protection from harm. But maybe God is protecting us from an unhealthy relationship or shielding us from an injury or near miss. Maybe our miracle is the moment we first look at our newborn's face. Or maybe it's found in a friend caring enough to be our voice of reason when we're about to make a big mistake.

I pray that we would have a willing heart like Naaman's servant girl, allowing ourselves to be an instrument that would provide blessing and healing ... and maybe even be a vessel for a miracle in someone else's life.

Pray With Me

Lord Jesus, Your presence soothes my soul. It changes me. I pray that my legacy will be that I am a woman of great faith who walked in the power of the Holy Spirit. Show me your everyday miracles, Lord. Help me not to miss seeing Your power in my life. Give me the faith to expect miracles, the strength to live in victory, and experience the full life You desire for me. In Jesus' name, amen.

Do not let your hearts be troubled. You believe in God; believe also in me. My Father's house has many rooms; if that were not so, would I have told you. that I am going there to prepare a place for you? And if I go and prepare a place for you, I will come back and take you to be with me that you also may be where I am. John 14:1-3

Questions for Reflection / Thoughts to Ponder

1. What has God done for you that changed you to where you were never the same?

2. What can you do today to walk in the power of the Holy Spirit?

3. Which one of Jesus' miracles means the most to you and why?

14

LAYING IT DOWN

*As for me, I call to God, and the
Lord saves me. Evening, morning
and noon, I cry out in distress, and
he hears my voice. Psalm 55:16-17*

As you know by now, I have experienced loss in my life. But nothing prepared me for the day I said goodbye to Matthew. Everything changed that day. It affected every aspect of my life — from our family dynamic to our circle of friends, to my financial status, to my physical body, and a host of other changes.

Perhaps the hardest thing I've ever done is tell our boys that their daddy had gone to be with Jesus. I gathered them all in my bedroom. After I told them, my oldest son (13) looked like he wanted to hit something and stalked off. My second son (10) was silent. And the youngest (8) cried, "No! I don't want to be a family of four." For a long time, when we talked about doing something as a family, he would remind us that we couldn't do it because daddy wasn't with us.

We sat on my bed and held each other, wondering what our lives would be like without him. Our sense of security was gone. Our confidence drained. Our routine turned upside down.

Although going through a sudden tragedy, or a long illness that finally takes your loved one is extremely difficult, for me, it's the day-to-day living without your spouse that is the most painful. Words of comfort that tell you he's in a better place do not comfort.

Memories, though, can warm your heart and give you a sense of calmness. God alone gives you peace, but sometimes God is the last place people look. Whether we reach out to Him or not, He is there with us. God gives us peace. He takes on what weighs us down. He gives us joy.

The Battle to Surrender

I prayed "Lord, I surrender to you today" during my quiet time one morning in the Spring of 2022. I wrote the scripture "in all your ways, submit to him, and he will make your paths straight" (Proverbs 3:6) in my journal.

Then I remembered something I was supposed to text to a friend, so I immediately went to Facebook to find the link. And just like that, I surrendered the next 20 minutes to Facebook. Just got sucked in. Lord, help me!

How often do we decide to do something else instead of spending time with God? We don't mean to — after all, keeping up with family and friends can be a good thing. However, allowing that something to take precedence over the Lord . . . not so much. It may not be social media, but a movie binge, or even cleaning the house over spending time with the Lord (remember Martha?). Sometimes we try to study or have quiet time, but the constant buzzing of our phones holds us captive to another master.

Just to be clear, cleaning the house isn't wrong, and social media in moderation isn't sinful, but the trick comes in the balance. Which are we doing more of? How engaged are our hearts with the Lord in those "non-spiritual" activities? How can we bring the Lord with us while doing mundane daily tasks?

It's a battle to truly surrender but that's what we're called to do.

Submit yourselves, then, to God. Resist the devil, and he will flee from you. James 4:7

Part of us — our new, redeemed self — wants to trust and obey. But the "old self, also known as the flesh" fights against that submission. It pops up and tempts us through everyday distractions and confusion about the Scriptures. Our goal as a believer should be to walk more and more in the Spirit and less and less according to our fleshly nature.

For me, surrender is like a see-saw. One moment I'm up walking in the Spirit, fully committed, and experiencing that deep peace from God. The next, I'm down walking mostly according to my mind, will, and emotions, and living outside the power of the Holy Spirit. Living in the power of the Holy Spirit requires obedience and intentionality.

Surrender brings many benefits with it, too. When we surrender, we are rewarded with peace. Surrender calms our anxious hearts. It relieves us of the pressures of life. It allows us to experience the presence of Jesus. It gives us permission to laugh and smile and reflect Jesus. It clears the clutter in our minds so we can hear the Lord's voice. It provides a revelation in our own hearts of who we are in Christ. And it opens the door for us to be taught by Christ.

Let us strive for a life of surrender rather than to short-lived pleasures or distractions. And let us trust the timing of the One who redeems and gives us purpose.

Humble yourselves, therefore, under God's mighty hand, that he may lift you up in due time. 1 Peter 5:6

God Gives Us Peace in the Valley

A story from the book of Daniel illustrates peace in a real valley. King Nebuchadnezzar had a golden image built and required all people to bow down and worship it when they heard the sound of the horn, flute, and other instruments. Whoever failed to worship the image would be thrown into a blazing furnace.

When three Jews — Shadrach, Meshach and Abednego — were thrown into the fire for refusing to bow down to the king's image, they went in peace. Only God could give them the kind of calmness required to walk through that fire. They boldly went in because they weren't alone in the fire. They had faith God was able to deliver them, and if He didn't, they would still refuse to serve Nebuchadnezzar's gods.

God goes through what we go through. He's right there, walking through the fire with us. He encourages us to keep going. He takes our best efforts and makes something beautiful with it, turning them into His glory.

Consider Leah's story in Genesis 29 and how she learned to let go and find peace. The chapter covers the birth of her four boys - Reuben, Simeon, Levi, and Judah.

Reuben's name carried the message, "It is because the Lord has seen my misery." The name Simeon had a similar meaning. "Because the Lord heard that I am not loved." There was hope in the name given Levi. "Now at last my husband will become attached to me, because I have born him three sons." And then there was Judah. "This time I will praise the Lord."

What happened when she had her fourth son? I believe that after being the wife that was unloved and unwanted, Leah finally came to the point of contentment. When she let go, she was able to praise the Lord.

In Luke 7:36-50, a woman who had lived a sinful life brought an alabaster jar of perfume and wiped Jesus' feet with her hair. She came in tears and humility. She left in peace.

Luke 8 tells us the story of a woman who had been subject to bleeding for 12 years. Desperate, she sought Jesus at all costs. She was instantly healed when she touched the edge of Jesus' cloak. She came hopeful and humble. She left healed and in peace.

Jesus Takes on What Weighs Us Down

WE'VE GOT A PROBLEM

After getting three boys in bed, plus a few cousins one Thanksgiving night, (so my sister and mom could start Black Friday shopping at 5 am — yikes!) I finally settled in for the night. Shortly after, I was startled by a creeaaaaak and then what sounded like a loud knock. Well, frightened out of my mind is a more accurate statement.

I jumped up and opened the bedroom door to find nothing there. Then I remembered. I had packed up old baby clothes the weekend before and placed the boxes on the top shelf of our closet. I even wondered at the time if I had put too much weight on that shelf.

I didn't have to wonder anymore. The only words that came to mind when I saw the condition of the closet was "we've got a problem." The sound was from the screw slowly easing out of the wall. Then the pole holding the hanging clothes sagged because of lack of support. To my amazement, the shelf had not come down completely. But it was only a matter of time.

That shelf can be a lot like our lives. We stack up so much on ourselves that eventually we break. We can't hold up all the stuff on our plates. We can't sustain ourselves under the activities and obligations that weigh us down.

We need to take down every piece and hand it to Jesus. We need to give it to the One who has the strength to hold it all up.

Therefore, since we are surrounded by such a great cloud of witnesses, let us throw off everything that hinders and the sin that so easily entangles, and let us run with perseverance the race marked out for us. Hebrews 12:1

BURDENS ARE LIFTED AT CALVARY

On reading *God Calling* [1] one morning, two simple questions convicted me. "How can you be overwhelmed when I am with you? Why do you carry two days' burdens on the one day?"

Isn't that just like us? We can't just worry about one day, we take on worrying about the next . . . and the next and the next. It is a daily struggle to leave those burdens at the cross.

As I worried out loud about the possibility of rain on the day of an outdoor engagement party we were planning, my mom spoke with wisdom. "I'm just going to let the Lord decide. If He wants it to rain, it will rain. If not, it won't."

That stopped me in my tracks, and I left with that response on my mind. So simple. How often do I forget who is Lord in my life and assume I can change the outcome? My worry doesn't change one thing for the good. It just causes harm to me internally as well as physically. Oh, that I would take that approach to everything — just let God decide. He's going to anyway. I only need to be available when He wants me to do something, open to what He has to say, and ready to act when I get the word from Him.

1 Peter 5 tells us to give Him our worries.

Cast all your anxiety on him because he cares for you. Be alert and of sober mind. Your enemy the devil prowls around like a roaring lion looking for someone to devour. 1 Peter 5:7-8

"And my Spirit remains among you. Do not fear." Haggai 2:5

May God help us to refrain from borrowing burdens from tomorrow, but to seek His face and live our life in God's power, presence, and purpose.

Release your worries and stresses to Jesus. Ask Him to join you in your day today, to be in every moment, every circumstance — even every conversation. Place your cares and fears and worries in His hands.

LOOSEN YOUR HOLD

It was late May at the beach. My son was two and he had a death grip on me.

I remember that trip vividly. It was two months before I delivered our youngest child into the world. Garrett loved the wet, packed sand near the water. But he would not let his tiny feet touch the coarse, dry sand that covered most of the beach.

Big and pregnant, I carried him on my hip the length of sandy shores to the boardwalk that led to our condo. He would not budge, holding on as if his life depended on it.

The scene reminds me of those clip-on koala bear toys. Once he was attached to my hip, he was there to stay.

I don't know what fear kept him from walking — fear that kept him from truly enjoying the beach — but I waddle-walked him through the loose sand.

God has blessings He wants to give us. What Father doesn't want to give His children gifts that will bless them and help them succeed? And we desperately want the blessings He has for us. However, many of us have such a tight grip on earthly treasures, we have no empty hands left to accept them. God holds out His hand in love, but we miss the blessing.

Do we need to loosen our hold on some of the things in this world? It could be an object or person, or it could even be a care or worry we can't seem to let go of.

Remember the Lord is the giver of good gifts.

Every good gift and every perfect gift is from above, coming down from the Father of lights, with whom there is no variation or shadow due to change. James 1:17 (ESV)

Let's loosen our hold and live in joy and with the blessings God wants to give us.

Jesus Gives Us Joy for our Souls

"Everybody stay away! I'm highly infectious!"

On my "hundredth" boy scout summer camp with my youngest son, he began to itch. Not uncommon when you're camping out in the woods. However, after a while, I began to think it was something more than an insect bite or poison ivy. As much as I hated to leave the Louisiana summer heat for the cool air-conditioned doctor's office, we left the woods and headed to town.

His rash was highly contagious but since his clothing covered it, we were able to go back to camp where he immediately proclaimed his infection status. He got the terminology wrong, but we all knew what he meant and got a laugh out of it.

Oh, that we would be infectious in other ways.

A person may have an infectious or contagious personality. I have a friend who displays enthusiasm in her smile. When she smiles, you want to smile too. I have another friend, also a widow, who brightens the room when you're with her. Her energy and her passion for life come through in every conversation. You just want to be around people like this, who love life and see it as an adventure. I imagine Paul's leadership, sense of purpose, and zest for life influenced many to follow Christ.

That we could let go and enjoy every moment, live life to its fullest. No matter our calling, Jesus is the source of joy for our souls. Let that carry over to how we speak to and treat each other.

LAUGH AGAIN

I wrote "Laugh every day" as one of my New Year's resolutions in 2022. Yep, right up there with lose 15 pounds and write an encouraging note to someone every week. Crazy to think that I need to remind myself to laugh. But with my tendency to stress and worry, it fit.

Sitting in my favorite chair with a cup of tea in hand, I researched Bible verses about laughter during my morning devotion. A quick search also informed me of the health benefits of laughter. What did I learn? That I need to stop taking myself so seriously and laugh more.

Sometimes that's easier said than done. After the loss of a loved one, holidays especially can be downright depressing. I try to stay upbeat but they can get me down. I miss what I no longer have. I grieve for my boys because they've missed the influence of their dad. Seeing others enjoy holidays with ALL their family can sometimes trigger a downward spiral.

Have you been there? Are you sleepless from worry? Remember, worry doesn't change tomorrow — it only robs today of its joy. As the waves roll back out to sea, release your worries to Christ.

Maybe you've lost your joy, and laughter is a rare occurrence in your life.

Be careful, or your hearts will be weighed down with carousing, drunkenness and the anxieties of life. Luke 21:34

My husband loved to laugh. I mean, frequent belly laughs. He teased, he laughed, he smiled. He loved being with people and laughing with people. I, on the other hand, have resorted to reminding myself — in writing — to laugh.

Oh, but it's good to laugh. Research says that not only is laughter a result of comic relief, but it provides stress relief, among other health benefits. It's good for us spiritually, emotionally, and physically. While high-stress levels disrupt our sleep — leaving us too revved up to sleep — laughter can bust up that stress and bolster us into getting a better night's sleep.

Solomon wrote in Proverbs "A cheerful heart is good medicine, but a crushed spirit dries up the bones." This "medicine" is free and available anywhere, anytime, and to anyone. (Proverbs 17:22).

There's a reason God placed words about joy and laughter in the Bible. There's a reason He asks us to trust Him in all things. We can claim the promise that our sadness and tears can turn into laughter (Luke 6:21); our worries and fears can turn into trust and joy (Psalm 56:3-4).

Let's allow ourselves moments of joy, moments to live and enjoy the beauty around us. Let's thank Him for the blessings He's placed before us, the memories He allows to sustain us. Let's ask Him to fill our mouths with laughter and our tongues with songs of joy.

Funny thing is, now every laugh reminds me of the promise I made to myself. And that brings joy to my soul.

I encourage you to live and treasure today. Be fully conscious and be thankful for God-given moments to laugh and de-stress. Give it a try. Allow yourself moments of joy and laughter.

Restore the joy in your life and renew your mind . . . and laugh.

Pray With Me

Lord, I give You my anxious heart today. I release my burdens, fears, and anxieties to You. They only cause me physical illness and injury. I give them to the One who can handle it all. I trust You, wholeheartedly, with everything I have within me. Lord help me to release every worry, fear, heartache, and crushed spirit to You every day. In Jesus' name, amen.

You turned my wailing into dancing; you removed my sackcloth and clothed me with joy, Psalm 30:11

A cheerful heart is good medicine, but a crushed spirit dries up the bones. Proverbs 17:22

Blessed are you who hunger now, for you will be satisfied. Blessed are you who weep now, for you will laugh. Luke 6:21

Questions for Reflection / Thoughts to Ponder

1. What fear or worry do you need to lay down before Jesus today?

2. What burdens are you carrying today? Meditate on 1 Peter 5:7-8.

3. What makes you smile? Write down some of your God-given

moments of laughter and keep them close to your heart.

---

1. Russell, A. J. (Ed.). (1972, January). God Calling.

15

TURNING POINTS

I will instruct you and teach you in
the way you should go; I will guide
you with my eye. Psalm 32:8

Turning points, or times of decision, can significantly affect the trajectory of the rest of our lives. God is there for us during those times, however, sometimes God is the last place people look. We need to make sure our decisions are based on seeking God in prayer.

As soon as Judas took the bread, Satan entered into him. John 13:27

This was Judas' moment of decision. He chose to betray Christ, allowing the evil one into his life.

In contrast, Mary of Bethany demonstrated she treasured her relationship with Jesus more than her earthly treasures when she anointed Him with expensive ointment. Judas traded his relationship with

Christ for 30 pieces of silver and demonstrated his treasure was in earthly things.

What are your turning points — when we take a step one way or another? I remember the day I left the women's retreat I wrote about in a previous chapter. I had a strong desire to help other women experience what I experienced that weekend. I wanted to write down my story, whether I ever shared it with someone else or not. God used that time to help me heal.

Another turning point could be the day a person decides to become bitter against a person or against God. For some, it could be the decision to take that first drink or first smoke or to use that first vulgar word.

While the power in the world will try to influence us to do evil, we need to remember that the power that is in us is greater than the power in the world. (1 John 4:4)

We don't know much about Judas' personal walk — whether he was a believer that lost his way, or whether he never truly followed Christ. Or maybe he thought he could do his part, collect a reward, and Jesus would miraculously escape as he had done before. No matter the circumstance, he was faced with a decision, and he chose evil.

Go Forward Fearlessly

Fear is an interesting emotion. David was fearless when it came to saving a lamb from a lion and fighting Goliath. But when he heard about his son Absalom starting a conspiracy to take the throne, he fled.

Then David said to all his officials who were with him in Jerusalem, "Come! We must flee, or none of us will escape from Absalom. We must leave immediately, or he will move quickly to overtake us and bring ruin on us and put the city to the sword. 2 Samuel 15:14

But David continued up the Mount of Olives, weeping as he went;
his head was covered and he was barefoot. All the people with
him covered their heads too and were weeping as they went up.
2 Samuel 15:30-31

Where did his courage go?

With Peter, the opposite happened. Peter was weak. Remember the rooster crowing experience? (On the day Jesus was arrested, He told Peter before the rooster crows, Peter would deny him three times.)(Luke 22:34) Just as Jesus said, the rooster crowed after Peter disowned Jesus three times. In that moment of denying Jesus, his heart must have sunk.

Are we sickened when we realize how our acts of disobedience pain Jesus? Judas was seized with remorse after he betrayed Jesus. He told the chief priests and elders he had sinned and betrayed innocent blood. He tried to give the thirty silver coins back, but they wouldn't take them back. Sadly, Judas then went and committed suicide because of his guilt.

When we sin, God certainly forgives us. We should not walk around feeling condemned. However, sin opens the door to the enemy in our lives and can lead to negative consequences that we may have to deal with for years to come.

Peer pressure and comparing ourselves to others can often cause us to make the wrong decision at certain critical moments in our lives.

Pilot experienced the greatest peer pressure of all time in his moment of decision. He resisted for a short time, but he ultimately wouldn't go against the pressure from the mob. Luke tells us Pilate decided to grant their demand. (Luke 23:24)

In comparison, Peter went on to be a leader and powerhouse for the Lord. I'd like to think he left that fear at the cross. He served the Lord with confidence, determination, and courage . . . except when newly converted Saul knocked on the door. According to the book of Acts, they were all afraid of him, except Barnabas. That day, Barnabas was the bold one! He brought Paul to the disciples. (Acts 9:26)

Sometimes boldness means taking drastic action for a breakthrough. The Bible describes many people who were desperate for change.

Desperate Faith Transforms

He was desperate.

Zacchaeus wanted to see Jesus so intensely, he climbed a tree to look for Him above the crowd. He risked his reputation and his standing in the community to see for himself what others were talking about. He was transformed after one visit with Jesus, giving half his possessions to the poor and giving back over and above what he had cheated people.

Jacob was also desperate. He wrestled through the night to receive a blessing.

Desperate to provide for her mother-in-law, Ruth was devoted, diligent, grateful, and obedient.

Hannah was desperate when she begged God for a child. In her great anguish and grief, she poured out her soul to the Lord. She made her request, worshipped the Lord, and went home. Later, she gave birth and named him Samuel, saying "Because I asked the Lord for him."

Esther was desperate for the welfare of her people, standing in the gap for them. Her faith resulted in the salvation of the Jewish people.

And so was Mary. She sat at Jesus' feet, soaking in his words, leaving her chores, and casting her to-do lists aside. Did she sense something that Martha didn't? That she only had a short time with Jesus and wanted to make the most of it?

DESPERATION'S TRANSFORMING POWER

Are we desperate? Paul admonishes us to be transformed by the renewing of our minds in Romans 12.

Do we really want to be transformed? Do we really want to discover and walk in God's will for our lives? How desperate are you for a turning point in your life? The book of Hebrews tells us that God rewards those who diligently seek Him. (Hebrews 11:6)

Abraham experienced transforming power. Against all odds, he placed his hope in God and believed He would do what He said.

Ours can be a transforming faith too. The Bible says we are more than conquerors through Christ who loves us (Romans 8:37). Our faith can stand the tests and temptations that come our way.

King Solomon was tested. The Queen of Sheba heard about his relationship with the Lord in 1 Kings 10. She came with great fanfare to test him with hard questions. Solomon answered everything with great wisdom. His wisdom exceeded what she had heard. Matter of fact, the scripture says she was overwhelmed.

People will test us too. Some of us may be tempted to turn away from God, but the truth is, who would we run to? God alone is the one who can meet our needs and fill the longing of our souls.

Let them give thanks to the LORD for his unfailing love and his wonderful deeds for mankind, for he satisfies the thirsty and fills the hungry with good things. Psalm 107:8-9

Experience God

What is your turning point? Let us seek God and experience God. Everything is fine when I'm sitting comfortably in my home writing down my thoughts. It's when I'm living outside of my pen and chair that I falter. The days when I fail to show grace to my kids. Days when I don't follow through on a commitment, or when I turn a deaf ear to God's prompting.

In his book *The Circle Maker*,[1] Mark Batterson challenges us to seek God above everything else. "If you seek answers, you won't find them, but if you seek God, the answers will find you."

God is not hiding. Keep seeking Him and let Him wrap His arms around you. Allow His presence to wash over you. Live with joy and experience all that He has for you and commit not to miss anything from this day forward. I have to remind myself of these things weekly, sometimes daily. Often, it's a one-step forward, two steps back kind of world, but God calls us to keep moving forward.

I pray that you will fulfill His calling for you, that you would not hold back, but step out in faith to live the life God intended for you. Neale Donald Walsch, known for *The Conversations with God*[2] series once said, "Life begins at the edge of your comfort zone."

I encourage you to pray for wisdom every day. Don't regret or worry about what happened yesterday or stress over what is to come tomorrow, but focus on today only.

HE IS DOING A NEW THING

With your recent loss, you may sense a lack of purpose. But God does have a purpose for your life. He often has good things for us right around the corner when we're wondering if we can make it one more day! I imagine that's how David felt while hiding from Saul in a cave. David cried out to God, acknowledging that God fulfills His purpose for David. (Psalm 57:2)

Certainly, He is doing a new thing in us too.

"Forget the former things; do not dwell on the past. See, I am doing a new thing! Now it springs up; do you not perceive it? Isaiah 43:18-19

These good things could be new plans to get us to that purpose. We need His guidance more than ever. David also called God his rock and fortress; asking God to lead him and guide him. (Psalm 31:3)

May this be true in our lives today.

Experience Forgiveness

God has called me to forgive many times during my life. When I've been hurt by someone, I know I must forgive to be able to move on. God knows I tend to live my life in the past rehashing moments and events, words I've used, mistakes I've made, actions I've taken, or dwelling on things that have been taken or said against me. Guilt over what I could have or should have done differently eats at me.

My husband lived life to the full and without regrets. I've always wanted that to be my mantra, but it has not come so easily for me over the years. Even after his death, I remembered every unkind word, thought, or deed I had or did against him. I wished a thousand times that I'd been a better wife to him. I wished I had focused more on his strengths and not on what I wanted to change. As I've missed him, I've wished I had done things differently.

But as I've thought about how he lived with no regrets, I know that's how he would want me to live too.

So, God has called me to forgive once again. This time . . . to forgive myself. Over the years, I've had to forgive others so I could move on and have joy in my life. I have made many mistakes, but I believe God does not want me to live in the past, but to put aside thoughts of the past and live for today . . . for what He has for me at this moment in my life.

Brothers and sisters, I do not consider myself yet to have taken hold of it. But one thing I do: Forgetting what is behind and straining toward what is ahead, I press on toward the goal to win

the prize for which God has called me heavenward in Christ Jesus.
Philippians 3:13-14

Start Fresh

Going through a season of grief after great loss is normal, but God doesn't want you to stay there. If I have learned anything during this season, it's that God provides us with what we need to make it through this time of grief and His love, mercy and faithfulness never ends.

The steadfast love of the Lord never ceases; his mercies never come to an end; they are new every morning; great is your faithfulness.
Lamentations 3:22-23 (ESV)

On a dark country backroad in the Rocky Mountains of New Mexico, I drove in awe at the clear, starry January night around me. Living in Louisiana with its towering trees, I rarely get to see the sun as it begins its climb. How I wanted to get to a place where I could see it rise over the flat New Mexico terrain.

The sky began to lighten in the East and gradually the stars lost their brilliance. Leaving the mountainous area, I could see the sky turn orange. As I stopped atop a small hill to watch its final entrance, all other light took a backseat.

The quietness and stillness of the morning did not escape me. The rising of the sun did not disappoint.

Why do I love to see sunrises and sunsets so much? Would I take them for granted if I lived on the coast somewhere? I hope not. There's something about the beginning of a new day or the ending of the day that brings hope for a new beginning and encouragement to face what's ahead.

And wow, did I need hope for a new beginning at that moment in early January of 2021. In the aftermath of the pandemic of 2020 and the realization that I did not accomplish the goals I had set for myself (again), I hoped for a different outcome in the year to come. According to author Rick Warren in his book *The Purpose Driven Life*,[3] "Hope is as essential to your life as air and water.

> "You need hope to cope." – Rick Warren in *The Purpose Driven Life*

The sunrise that day was a reminder of God's great love for me, and that each day is an opportunity to start fresh. In the same way, the book of Lamentations reminds us that God's mercies are new every morning and that He is faithful. Not just faithful, but great is His faithfulness (Lamentations 3:22-23 (ESV)). Let that sink in. We cannot even comprehend that kind of steadfast, trustworthy, never-leave-you kind of faithfulness.

My prayer is that we would trust in the faithfulness of our Creator and put our hope in the Lord. The words of an old 1980's Gabriel song, *I Put My Hope,* ring true. When we put our trust in Christ, we will not be shaken. We can trust that he will see us through any trial in our lives.

I want to trust in His plan for my day and ask for His guidance. I can do nothing about yesterday and I certainly can't control what comes my way, but I can place my hope and trust in Jesus Christ today.

Let's look to each day as a gift and opportunity to place our hope in Jesus and honor Him with our trust.

Pray With Me

Jesus, You are my Rock and Redeemer. I will not fear for You are with me. I will trust in You and put my hope in You. Thank You that we don't have to dwell on the mistakes or pain of yesterday because Your mercies are new every morning. Every day is a gift. Help me to live my life with that truth in mind. In Jesus' name, amen.

———————————— 🎩 ————————————

The LORD bless you and keep you; the LORD make his face to shine upon you and be gracious to you; the LORD turn his face toward you and give you peace. Numbers 6:24-26

I wait for the Lord, my whole being waits, and in his word I put my hope. Psalm 130:5

I will not forget you! See, I have engraved you on the palms of my hands. Isaiah 49:15-16

From the rising of the sun to the place where it sets, the name of the LORD is to be praised. Psalm 113:3

Let us hold unswervingly to the hope we profess, for He who promised is faithful. Hebrews 10:23

"Blessed is the man who trusts in the Lord, and whose confidence is in him." Jeremiah 17:7

For if you forgive other people when they sin against you, your heavenly Father will also forgive you. Matthew 6:14

And when you stand praying, if you hold anything against any-one, forgive them, so that your father in heaven may forgive you your sins. Mark 11:25

Questions for Reflection / Thoughts to Ponder

1. What has been your biggest moment of decision and how did you respond?

2. What was the impact on you and others?

3. What would you have done differently?

---

1. Batterson, M. (2022, October 4). Circle Maker by Batterson, Mark [Hardcover]. Zondervan,2011.

2. Walsch, N. D. (1996, October 29). Conversations with God: An Uncommon Dialogue, Book 1 (Conversations with God Series) (1st ed.). TarcherPerigee.

3. Warren, R. (2013, December 31). The Purpose Driven Life: What on Earth Am I Here For? (10th Anniversary). Zondervan.

16

WITH JESUS, JOY REIGNS

"The God who made the world
and everything in it is the Lord of
heaven and earth and does not live
in temples built by human hands.
And he is not served by human
hands, as if he needed anything.
Rather, he himself gives everyone
life and breath and everything
else. Acts 17:24-25

I began running marathons by accident. My friend Angela had a goal to run one before she turned 40. I was 48 at the time. We ran that first one in Savannah, Georgia, and completed six marathons in three years, to my mother and mother-in-law's horror. I ran three in one year!

To train, we ran a half marathon first. Oh. My. Word. I was not even close to being prepared for that day. Let me tell you, training makes all the difference in the world.

After that, though, I knew what to expect and how to train. And then the adventure began. The hardest — but most successful — marathon for me was three weeks after my husband died. I almost canceled my participation but knew he would have been disappointed if I didn't follow through.

So I ran. Not long into the race, officials diverted the crowd of runners to two sides of the course. As I got closer, I saw the problem. A runner had collapsed. I couldn't believe it. How could I see someone in almost the same situation as my husband, who never recovered from that kind of fall? I prayed for him, then thought, "this is my undoing." As tears stung my eyes, I wanted to put my fists in the air and shout "this is not fair!"

Life's Not Fair

John 5 tells the story of a man, an invalid for 38 years, waiting for a dip in the pool at Bethesda. The problem? Every time he tried to get in, someone else beat him to it. Sick people gathered at this pool in hopes of being cured of their illnesses. They believed that the first person to step into the water after it was stirred by an angel was healed.

Life wasn't fair for this man. He had an opportunity to be healed, but he couldn't physically get to the pool in time.

Then Jesus approached and asked if he wanted to be well. He answered, "I have no one to help me in the pool when the water is stirred."

Jesus told him to pick up his mat and walk. In an instant, the man was cured. He picked up his mat and walked.

How often do we want to cry "it's unfair?"

When we're tempted to say, "life's unfair," we need to remember Jesus. He never cried in complaint. Never shouted it's unfair. He just did what he was called to do.

All of us will suffer at times. Life will absolutely knock us down sometimes. Satan still strikes, attempting to destroy us. But Jesus showed us how to be victorious. His Word gives us instructions for every area of our lives.

We never heard the result of that runner's fall. Since there was no word, we assumed the best outcome. God gave me the strength and courage to move past the pain, cross the finish line, and complete the race at my best time.

I chose to walk in victory and I hope you will too. We can experience victory because Jesus cares and when the time is right, he will tell us to pick up our mat and walk.

Finish Well

As I write the last words of this book, I pray that God will give me the strength and courage to finish well on the course He has for my life. I pray that for you, too. Wherever you are, whatever is next for you, may God grant you the wisdom and courage and strength to continue the course and finish strong.

Therefore, since we are surrounded by such a great cloud of witnesses, let us throw off everything that hinders and the sin that so easily entangles. And let us run with perseverance the race marked out for us. Hebrews 12:1

I pray that you would begin to know how wide and vast and deep His love is for you. I pray that you would get to know the Father as your true Heavenly Father, Jesus as your best friend, and the Holy Spirit as your comforter.

I hope that the ideas and encouragement presented here will help you discover joy in your season of pain and sorrow. When we strive to live our lives to the full, look for blessings in the pain, and surrender to Christ, there is an unspeakable joy and deep connection with the God who knows us. It certainly won't always be easy - and there will be painful reminders along the way, but Jesus has made a way to experience that type of joy — a joy rooted in a faith in Jesus Christ.

Experience a Firm Foundation

The thoughts written in this book come from a foundation in Jesus Christ. There is no possible way I could have endured this experience without the strength of my Lord. And I've never been more glad I put my faith in Jesus.

You may have grown up knowing the verses I've presented throughout this book and relating to the God moments I have shared.

However, the concepts presented here may also be foreign to some of you. You do not have that type of relationship with God and have never experienced the love of Jesus.

To tell you my story is to tell you of Him. It would be my greatest honor to take your hand, introduce you, and walk you through how to accept Jesus Christ as your Lord and have a personal relationship with Him.

God revealed His plan of salvation in the Holy Bible.

I believe the Holy Bible is the Word of God — without error — spoken to mankind.

I believe that the Godhead exists in three persons — God the Father, the Son (Jesus Christ), and the Holy Spirit.

I believe that Jesus Christ came down from Heaven, was born of a virgin, and lived a perfect life so we could know what God was like. He was mocked and crucified, hung on a cross to pay the price for the sins of mankind, and then rose from the dead three days later. He is our intercessor to God the Father.

Jesus Christ purchased our redemption through His death and resurrection. His offer of salvation is available to all who believe and receive.

For God so loved the world that he gave his one and only Son, that whosoever believes in him shall not perish but have eternal life.
John 3:16

Salvation is a gift of God's grace, received by faith in Christ alone.

For it is by grace you have been saved, through faith — and this is not from yourselves, it is the gift of God — not by works, so that no one can boast. Ephesians 2:8-9

Salvation involves recognizing that you are a sinner and repenting from your sin, confessing with your mouth, "Jesus is Lord," and believing in your heart that God raised Him from the dead. Salvation is received through personal faith in the Lord Jesus Christ. All who receive Him are changed by the Holy Spirit and literally are born again. They become children of God and receive eternal life with God.

because if you confess with your mouth that Jesus is Lord and believe in your heart that God raised him from the dead, you will be saved. Romans 10:9 (ESV)

For, "everyone who calls on the name of the Lord will be saved."
Romans 10:13 (ESV)

The Choice is Yours

There are two choices in this life. One is to receive the gift of salvation that leads to eternal life and a home in heaven. The other is to reject God's offer of salvation, leading to everlasting punishment for unbelievers in hell.

But our citizenship is in heaven. And we eagerly await a Savior from there, the Lord Jesus Christ. Philippians 3:20

Anyone whose name was not found written in the book of life was thrown into the lake of fire. Revelation 20:15

"Then they will go away to eternal punishment, but the righteous to eternal life." Matthew 25:46

"Then he will say to those on his left, Depart from me, you who are cursed, into the eternal fire prepared for the devil and his angels." Matthew 25:41

Jesus Calls You by Name

"Mary."

When she heard Him tenderly call her name, Mary's search for Jesus at the tomb was over. She had left close friends at home to search for Jesus' body, but what she found was Christ the risen Lord.

In his book, *Mornings with Tozer*, [1]A. W. Tozer says, "Christ's resurrection brought about a startling change of direction for the believers. Sadness and fear and mourning marked the direction of their religion before they knew that Jesus rose from the dead."

That direction changed with the sound of three simple phrases. "He is not here; He has risen, just as He said." That day, the followers of Jesus shifted their focus away from the tomb to the telling of the good news. He is risen indeed!

Tozer goes on to say, "Thankfully, the resurrection morning was only the beginning of a great, vast outreach that has never ended — and will not end until our Lord Jesus Christ comes back again!"

The Bible is the voice of God calling us to new life. Leaving our sinful life behind, we can live a new, redeemed life instead. Where we spend eternity depends on how we respond to that voice. My friend, is today the day to experience the power of Christ's resurrection?

For believers, Satan would have us linger beside the cross in mourning instead of proclaiming that Christ has risen. Because He lives and did not stay in the tomb, we can face whatever tomorrow holds. Because He lives, we can live without fear but with a sense of purpose and significance. Because He lives, we are called to act, to tell others about the saving power of Jesus.

For those who have not yet believed, is today the day to loosen your grip on the world and reach out to receive the salvation Jesus offers? He is also calling you to act, to accept His gift of eternal life, and to experience life to the full.

In John 10:10, Jesus reminds us that the thief comes to steal and kill and destroy. That same enemy wants to steal our joy . . . to rob us of the gift of knowing Jesus Christ. He wants to destroy our faith and have us feel hopeless and bound. He wants us to experience feelings of negativity, including doubt that God really loves us.

But . . .

Jesus also tells us in John 10:10 "I have come that you might have life and have it to the full."

For me, God stepped in and changed everything. It doesn't mean it's been easy. I've cried a river of tears. I've made countless mistakes. I've learned lessons the hard way.

But God still has more for me to accomplish, more joy to experience, and more life to live. I believe He has the same for you, too.

Walking through this season of suffering after your loss is probably one of the most difficult journeys of your life. If you are a believer, or if you are just now accepting His gift of salvation, you can live an abundant life as you walk this path of pain. You can receive blessings. You can find peace when you surrender to Him. There is no greater joy than what we will find in a relationship with Jesus.

Jesus is tenderly calling your name. With Him, you can live with joy again. You can live your life to its fullest.

In the marathon world, simply finishing the race is an accomplishment. What a thrill it is just to cross the finish line. Participants who finish all receive a finisher medal and certificate.

My friend, Jesus Christ is the author and finisher of our faith. He is the beginning and the end. He is the way, the truth, and the life. Jesus wants to set us free and give us an abundant, full life. And what a thrill it will be to someday cross over the finish line and see Him face to face.

Prayer of Salvation

Jesus, thank You for suffering for us, redeeming us from our sins. Thank you for Your perfect plan. I admit that I am a sinner and in need of your grace. I believe that You (Jesus) are the Son of God, lived a sinless life, shed your blood on the cross for my sins, and rose from the dead.

I humbly ask You to forgive me of my sins and receive me as a child of God. I make the decision to make You Lord of my life.

In the name of Jesus, Amen.

Now this is eternal life, that they may know you, the only true God, and Jesus Christ, whom you have sent. John 17:3

The Lord himself goes before you and will be with you; he will never leave you nor forsake you. Do not be afraid; do not be discouraged. Deuteronomy 31:8

In his last days, David said "If my house were not right with God, he would not have made with me an everlasting covenant, arranged and secured in every part, surely he would not bring to fruition my salvation and grant me my every desire. 2 Samuel 23:5

We believe it is through the grace of our Lord Jesus Christ that we are saved. Acts 15:11

You turned my wailing into dancing; you removed my sackcloth and clothed me with joy, that my heart may sing your praises and not be silent. LORD my God, I will praise you forever. Psalm 30:11-12

Questions for Reflection / Thoughts to Ponder

1. Think about your relationship with Jesus Christ. Are you living an abundant life? With Christ as Lord, you can. What steps do you need to take to make that happen?

2. Is today the day to loosen your grip on the world and reach out to receive salvation? Accept His gift of eternal life, and experience life to the full.

3. Jesus tenderly calls us by name. Take a moment and let that soak in. Be still and surrender to Him.

---

1. Tozer, A. W., & Smith, G. B. (2008). Mornings with Tozer: Daily Devotional Readings. Macmillan Publishers.

Acknowledgments

To my Lord and Savior Jesus Christ. Without my faith, I would be lost and without joy.

The Lord has surrounded me with many friends and family who have poured into my life and into this book project. Thank you for taking a chance on me. I am overwhelmed by your love and kindness.

In memory of my loving husband, Matthew. For the 20 years we knew each other, you were my best friend, my biggest supporter, and the one who made me laugh.

To my sons, Connor, Garrett, and Parker — you are my joy. We've walked this journey together. Nothing compares to being your mom.

To my parents, Sonny and Mattie Mercer, who taught me about God's faithfulness, no matter the circumstances. You have loved, supported, and listened even when you didn't know what I was doing.

To my father-in-law and mother-in-law, Syd and Sara Cameron — you have treated me as your own and blessed my life.

To Lisa Mencer, Sarah Heatherly, Elizabeth Cobb, Angela O'Dowd, Kimberly Stuckey, Aimee Kane, Christy McIntyre, Jennifer Douglas, Lee Mayronne, Amanda Hinton, and Leigh-Ann Cascio (and awesome photographer) — for being my sounding board. You believed in me and encouraged me to keep moving forward.

To (Aunt) Laura Boyd — my weekly encourager and top cheerleader

To my nephew James Mencer — for putting my last-minute song list together. You're awesome!

To Derek and Olga Koecher — I am forever grateful to you.

To Jason Byron Nelson — my cover designer, but also so much more. Thank you for listening to my ideas and for being patient with me. Your creativity inspires and amazes me. Plus, you're just fun to work with.

My beta readers — Paula Russell and Bobbie Stuckey. Thank you for your feedback and encouragement.

Matthew's business partners — Eric Weis, Jarod Stokes and Jeremy Cave — your Matthew stories warm my heart and make me laugh.

To my proofreaders — Lauren Cassel Brownell and Liz Craft. Your finishing touches pulled everything together.

To my Kickstarter backers who believed in this book. I am honored that you would back the project. (In order of when they backed) Mitzi Reed, Rhonda Ward, Chris Cobb, Laura Boyd, Jennifer Douglas, Beth Heatherly, Paula Russell, Lea Ann Winkle, Lee Trichel, Kamie Schnuelle, Terri Weeks, Bob Fudickar, Lisa Carey, Shauna Perez, Mike Maslowski, Pearl Wise, Cheryl Jacobo, William Meinel, Eugene Wick, Jeremy Cave, Marc Temple, Lisa Feldhaus, Quentin Messer Jr., Kristi Davis, Sonya Speir, Laurie Alm, Eric Weis, Renee Arrington, Clinton Whitney Downing, James Mencer, Christy Gray, Angela Odom, Debbie Smith, Nicole Brown, Christy, Bill Bradley, Anna Lisa Deal, Aimee Kane, Audrey Malloy, Stephanie Polk, Darlene Duncan, Ashley Herring, Eric Daniel Saulters-Wood, Jacqueline Powell, Mary, Vicky Sanders.

And to my Launch Team for your support and encouragement. You were amazing. Renee Arrington, Jennifer Bass, Melissa Batson, Adam Bricker, Nicole Brown, Monica Cagle, Julie Cain, Elizabeth Cobb, Kristi Davis, Tami Frazier, Debra Gammill, Sarah Heatherly, Carol Hendrix, Amanda Hinton, Teresa Howard, Aimee Kane, Lisa Keyes, Amanda May, Lee Mayronne, Mattie Mercer, Angela O'Dowd, Jacqueline Powell, Vicky Sanders, Rachel Shelby, Georgia Street, Kim Stuckey, Bonny Van, Johnna Van, Amy Weems, Marlene Williams, Lea Ann Winkle, Lana Wilson, Faren Wise. Special thanks to Clinton Downing.

About Author

Raised among the cypress trees and bayous of the Louisiana Delta, Patricia Cameron learned early on to cherish God and family. After her biggest trial tested her faith, she now aspires to help others see that God is worthy of praise, even in times of grief. Her late husband's zest for life inspired her to live her own fully aware of God's presence, power and purpose — and to encourage others to do the same. Patricia has the honor and joy of raising three sons, Connor, Garrett and Parker. She also cherishes her daughter Ashlynn, who died at birth and is safe in the arms of Jesus. *Grief Unwrapped: Discovering Joy in a Season of Sorrow,* is Patricia's first book.

You can find out more and sign up for her newsletter at patriciacam eronwrites.com.

f facebook.com/faithdrivenjoy

instagram.com/faithdrivenjoy

twitter.com/faithdrivenjoy

GRIEF UNWRAPPED PLAYLIST

1. Nothing Else | Cody Carnes

2. Here with Me | MercyMe

3. In the Waiting | Greg Long

4. There is Power in the Blood | Alan Jackson

5. The Solid Rock | Grace Community Church

6. In Christ Alone | Michael English

7. Trust in You | Lauren Daigle

8. Excuses | Kingsmen

9. Praise You In This Storm | Casting Crowns

10. Even If | MercyMe

11. Come Thou Fount | MercyMe

12. Remember to Remember | Steven Curtis Chapman

13. Tell Your Heart To Beat Again | Danny Gokey

14. Dancing in the Sky | Dani and Lizzy

15. One More Day | Diamond Rio

16. Banana Pancakes | Jack Johnson

17. Keep Going | The Revivalists

18. Because He Lives | David Crowder Band

19. Holy Water | We The Kingdom

20. Never Once | Matt Redman

21. I Put My Hope | Gabriel

22. Elijah | Rich Mullins

Dare to live for Jesus!

TAKE TIME TO LAUGH

Search for the joy in life.

You're at your wits end. And you've just run out of hope.

Where is God when you need Him the most? Whether you're in the battle of your life or in desperate need of a friend, *By My Side* meets you at the point of your need and helps you recognize the One who walks beside you. The One who is always by your side.

patriciacameronwrites.com

If the words in this book have helped you in some way, please post a review about it.